Wheatley Hills Golf Club

CENTENNIAL

1913 — 2013

Published by Stewart Commemorative Services — Manlius, New York 13104

Edited by Mary Jane BeVard

Designed by Daniel J. J. Cameron

Written by Perry Vascellaro, Richard Kearns, John A. Needham and Arlene Stewart

This limited edition book has been
published for the members of
The Wheatley Hills Golf Club
as part of the 100th anniversary of the Club.

ISBN: 978-0-9888029-0-2

FOREWORD

In 1913, a dedicated group of golf enthusiasts set out on a bold plan to establish and build a new golf course on the Titus farm in East Williston. They overcame many challenges and were steadfast in pursuit of the goal to create a first-class golf club to leave as their legacy. One hundred years later, Wheatley Hills Golf Club looks back at a rich and proud history as it celebrates its centennial year in 2013.

This book tells the story of Wheatley Hills, from its historic early days in rural Nassau County, its developing years in the 1920s and 1930s and its evolution as one of Long Island's premier golf courses. We reflect on the impact of legends like noted course architect Devereaux Emmet and master builder Robert Moses, to our own golf legends of Willie Klein, Jack Mallon and Gene Francis.

The Wheatley story is one of great golf and great people. We have attempted to capture both elements within these pages as we commemorate this momentous occasion. We honor our champions on the golf course as well as those who have served in leadership roles providing the foundation of a successful club. We acknowledge the many families who helped build our tradition. We take a look at life at Wheatley Hills over the years as captured in The Bell and relive many of our happy moments and traditions, along with our devastating fire in 1976.

A valuable outcome of the book's compilation is the documentation of archives and historical notes that we can now pass on to future generations of membership. We are deeply indebted to Perry Vascellaro and his committee of Park Adikes, John Needham and Dick Kearns, as well as our publisher, Arlene Stewart. They have devoted many hours of research in developing the content for this publication with the assistance of our Wheatley staff. We are also grateful to many of our fellow members who contributed their stories, memorabilia and photographs to this effort. They are formally acknowledged on the page titled Recognition.

We hope that our membership will be renewed with an even stronger sense of pride about all that Wheatley Hills has accomplished and the traditions it holds in high esteem. We continue to be bonded by our love of the game, our passion for the natural beauty of our course and an insatiable zest for life and friendship. On behalf of the Board of Governors, we thank all our members for their contributions to the success we have enjoyed together and look forward to continuing the Wheatley Hills traditions in the years to come.

William Poisson
President

DEDICATION

Encouraged by the love of golf and a vision to obtain land suitable for a golf course,
we dedicate this history of Wheatley Hills Golf Club in celebration of our 100-year anniversary
to the gentlemen who brought Wheatley Hills Golf Club into being on May 13, 1913:

RICHARD W. TURNER

HUGH E. O'REILLY   FRED W. WESTLAKE

EUGENE VAN SCHAICK   WILSON B. BRICE

GEORGE H. LOWDEN   GEORGE WOOLSTON

Included in this dedication are all the founding members who established the principles that have served us well for 100 years.
Their dedication and foresight have enabled Wheatley Hills to continually move forward and prosper.

TABLE OF CONTENTS

BEFORE WE WERE WHEATLEY HILLS

T he Long Island Motor Parkway was the vision of William K. Vanderbilt, Jr. The portion of the toll road nearest the Wheatley Hills Golf Course was built between 1908-1910 and by 1926, was extended all the way from Flushing to Lake Ronkonkoma.

Built originally as a racing venue and a limited-access concrete parkway, it was the first road built specifically for automobiles.

By 1911, six toll lodges were constructed with living accommodations for the gatekeepers and their families.

At the very same time in this rural community of Nassau County with a population of approximately 100,000 people (now 1.3 million), golf was becoming a popular pastime and several courses had already been developed in the Garden City area – Midland was an informal neighborhood club organized in 1899. The club's

This photo shows the Motor Parkway with undeveloped farmland on both sides. It was land similar to this that eventually became the home of Wheatley Hills Golf Club.

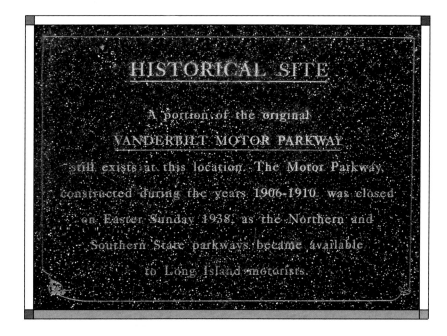

This plaque, recognizing where pieces of the Motor Parkway still exist, is located on the course behind the fourth tee.

This was the early version of heavy equipment.

members (men and women) maintained their own clubhouse and nine-hole golf course. After their course fell victim to real estate development, the Midland members played at Salisbury Links, but in 1912 they decided to build their own course in East Williston. They founded the Wheatley Hills Golf Club in 1913.

Mr. Titus had already sold over 68 acres of his farmland in order to allow Vanderbilt to build the roadway through this section of land. Accordingly, the Motor Parkway was built before the Wheatley Hills Golf Club was established.

Building a course when giant mechanical earth-moving equipment was not available was an impressive feat. Architect Robert Trent Jones estimated that it took seven teams of horses one week to contour a single green. This alone was a motivating force to the designer to be sure he got it right the first time out. Many designers would live on the property being designed for extended periods to assure their plans were followed.

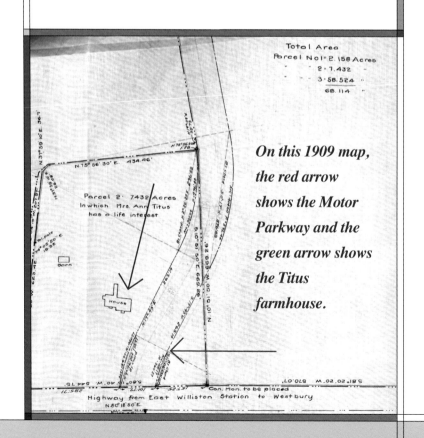

On this 1909 map, the red arrow shows the Motor Parkway and the green arrow shows the Titus farmhouse.

THE EARLY YEARS

T hrough its early years, the club's property was bisected by the Long Island Motor Parkway, which divided the golf course in two equal pieces. A map dated 1928 shows the parkway and the bridge that was built so golfers could get from one side of the golf course to the other.

The men who had the vision of a new golf course saw the land on both sides of the parkway as an ideal location since it would have no interruption of play for the members, from pedestrians, equestrians or vehicles, since not a single roadway or pathway crossed the land.

They considered the old fenced-in Motor Parkway an attraction, not a detriment and proceeded to make the arrangements to lease the farmland and the old Titus homestead.

An entrance to the Wheatley Hills Golf Club was also established with a discounted fee of $0.50 for club members and their guests.

The new organization struggled along with an obsolete clubhouse and rented grounds. Still, the founders had accomplished a grand feat. Wheatley Hills Golf Club was born into the golfing world. The name "Wheatley" chosen for the club dates back at least as far as the middle of the 18th century, and is familiar throughout nearby Old Westbury. Indeed, the land immediately to the west of the club was known as Wheatley Ridge.

The Wheatley Hills founding group consisted of about 40 men, former Salisbury players all, many of them members of the Midland Club.

They were joined shortly thereafter by another group of the same size, mostly Brooklynites, who had tried unsuccessfully to organize the Glenwood Country Club.

The "movement away from Salisbury" was led by R.W. Turner, the club's first president. The story of the progress of the Wheatley Hills Golf Club at East Williston, L.I. is an interesting one, especially to those who had the administrative responsibilities of the golf club affairs.

Original entrance from the Motor Parkway into the Wheatley Hills property.

IN WITNESS WHEREOF, we have hereunto set our hands and seals, the 13th day of May, 1913.

Hugh E. O'Reilly

Fred N. Westlake

Geoge H Lowden

Eugene Van Schaick

Wilson B Brice

-of-

WHEATLEY HILLS GOLF CLUB, INC.

WE, the undersigned, all being natural persons of full age, four of us being citizens of the United States and all of us being residents of the State of New York, being desirous of forming a membership corporation, do hereby certify as follows:

1. The name of the proposed corporation is WHEATLEY HILLS GOLF CLUB, INC.

2. The territory in which its operations are to be conducted is East Williston, in the Town of North Hempstead, Nassau County, State of New York.

3. The City in which its principal office is to be located is the City of New York, Borough of Manhattan.

4. The number of its governors is seven.

5. The names and places of residence of the persons to be its governors until its first annual meeting, to be held on the second Thursday of January, 1914, are as follows:-

NAMES.	PLACES OF RESIDENCE.
Richard W. Turner,	Garden City, Long Island.
Hugh E. O'Reilly,	Garden City, Long Island.
Fred W. Westlake,	197 Ocean Avenue, Brooklyn, N.Y.
Eugene Van Schaick,	The Ansonia, New York City.
Wilson B. Brice,	111 West 77th St., New York City
George H. Lowden,	Hempstead, Long Island.
George Woolston,	Garden City, Long Island.

We had four-ball tournaments as early as 1921.
These three are documented as September 30, 1921.

James Crossan, our third professional, is seen taking a swing in this 1919 photo. He is also shown in the upper right photo, hitting the ball.

They engaged golf course architect Devereaux Emmet to design an 18-hole golf course. Using their layout, Emmet had nine holes ready for play by the fall of 1913, and the full course completed by the following year. The bunkering was added in 1916. The original course was a par-74 test of 6022 yards, and in true Emmet style featured significant carriers over deep rough to reach the fairways. The first nine holes were built at a cost of $5,000.

Devereaux Emmet, world-renowned golf course architect, designed Wheatley Hills.

THE BROOKLYN DAILY EAGLE. NEW YORK, FRIDAY, JUNE 5, 1914.

FROM QUEENS BOROUGH AND ALL LONG ISLAND

WHEATLEY HILLS HAS FINE NEW GOLF CLUB

Home of New Country Club at
East Williston Being Put in Shape.

HAVE MANY NEW MEMBERS.

Eighty From Glenwood Country Club
Go Over to New Club—Has Two
Nine-Hole Courses

(Special to The Eagle.)
East Williston, L I., June 5—
With its membership increased by
about eighty members of the
Glenwood Country Club, which
recently disbanded, the-newly formed
Wheatley Hills Golf Club has made
extensive improvements to its
clubhouse and grounds here and has
become one of the important country
clubs in this section of Long Island.
The home of the club is just east of
this village and includes several farms
lying on both sides of the Motor
Parkway with an old-fashioned
country homestead made over for the
purposes of a clubhouse.
Nine holes of the golf course are
now in use and the other nine holes
will be ready in September.

A notable feature of the course is
that it included two distinct nine-
hole courses, one lying on each
side of the Motor Parkway, and
each beginning and ending at the
clubhouse. The land west of the
parkway is rather rolling, while
that on the east side is com-
paratively level so that the two
together provide an eighteen-hole
course of over. 6,000 yards with
a pleasing variety of ground. The
two courses are connected by a
passage under the parkway
between the ninth hole and tenth
tee—north of the clubhouse and
about halfway up the course, a
bridge has also been built over
the parkway.
The clubhouse is a fine type of
old-fashioned country home, and
has been made over into a very
pleasant clubhouse. It stands on
an elevation over the surrounding
land and about seven acres of
lawn on all sides dotted with
handsome shade trees.

Richard W. Turner is president of
the club. George H. Lowden is
secretary and Hugh E. O'Reilly is
treasurer. Others on the board of
governors are Eugene VanSchaick,
Wilson B. Brice, George Woolston
and Fred W. Westlake. The
property is held by the Wheatley
Hills Holding Company Inc. of
which the directors are;
Richard W. Turner, Hugh E.
O'Reilly, Fred Westlake, Wilson
B.Brice, Donald McKellar,
Eugene Van Schaick, and George
Lowden.
It is proposed to limit the membership to 300 and it is expected that
the list will fill rapidly. The
accessibility of the course, both by
the Long Island Railroad and by
automobile route from Brooklyn
and Manhattan, make it especially
popular.

HOME OF THE NEWLY FORMED
WHEATLEY HILLS
GOLF CLUB AT
EAST WILLISTON, L. I.

The new golf club on Long Island was big news in Brooklyn, since many of the members of the newly formed Wheatley Hills Golf Club were from there. It was a main story in the Sports section of the Brooklyn Eagle newspaper on June 5, 1914. A transcript of that story appears on the left.

The Titus farmhouse, a white, two-story, Southern Colonial structure situated to the north of the present clubhouse, served as Wheatley Hills' first home. An old ship bell, located behind the house and used to signal farm workers at mealtime and the end of the workday, is the only reminder of that period. Now located behind the practice putting green, it once was used to salute the victor in the club's championship tournament, and now serves as a significant symbol of the club.

The club purchased the land in 1926 and was able to use about $13,000, which had accumulated in the reserve fund, toward the cost of completing the new clubhouse. Further, it was possible during the previous fiscal year to avoid borrowing any money, as

Well-dressed spectators enjoy a match at the newly formed Wheatley Hills Golf Club in 1914.

temporary advances were made from the reserve fund, thus saving interest charges.

The property, which the club now owned, was occupied several years under lease with the privilege of purchase at a fixed valuation. In addition to paying the rent, the club took care of the taxes, insurance and other items, in all a considerable amount. When the purchase of the property was finally decided upon, naturally the most important phase of the situation was to finance the transaction. The purchase price, $145,000, was at length secured through the sale of $300 membership certificates and the issue of $66,000 in bonds out of an authorized issue of $150,000. It was obligatory for each member to purchase a membership certificate, provided he desired to remain in the club, such certificates being transferable through the club for resale to incoming members for the benefit of the holders.

THE NEW CLUB BUILDING

The well-known golf club architect, J.H. Phillips, designed the new Wheatley Hills Golf Clubhouse. An active golfer, Phillips made a special study of the design requirements. The new Wheatley Hills clubhouse would be of early American design. It was decided the exterior walls would be stone with a slate roof. A two-storied Colonial portico formed the entrance with a service wing rambling down the hill at the left and forming a forecourt. A high knoll at the right, occupied by the original clubhouse, which was dismantled, made the enclosure to the forecourt entrance on the right.

The northwesterly side of the building facing the course would have a veranda 75 feet long, with French windows opening from the main lounge, dining room and men's grill. Entrance to the locker room was designed to be directly in front of the first tee, and an outside staircase led down to the professional's room near the entrance to the locker room. The building was purposefully located with a view to give the easiest access possible to the course, also furnishing the most interesting views of the course from the veranda and all rooms of the club. New features would include a lounging space at the end of the locker room, as well as the quaint, homelike atmosphere of the interiors, rather than a hotel-like character.

The main entrance was on the ground floor through the Colonial portico entrance. The entrance opened into a large reception hall, with an office and stairway to the men's locker room at the left.

The ladies' reception and locker rooms were built to the right of the main entrance as was the main stairway to the general lounge and the main club floor. The professional's shop, chauffeurs' dining room, coatroom, valet, etc. were located at the westerly end of the ground floor, which would become the service end. The quarters for employees formed a wing, which acted as a screen for the service court.

The first floor reached from the reception hall, on the right, had a broad flight of stairs, to the general lounge. This room had a clear view to the roof, giving the height of a two-storied room with a large fireplace at the end and overlooking the 18th green. The large dining room adjoined the lounge, with windows in the portico just over the main entrance below. The men's grill adjoined the dining room, which also connected with the men's lounging room between the grill and the men's locker rooms, which occupied two floors. The new home was ready in May 1927.

In 1931, the club faced a crisis with the construction of the Northern State Parkway. The state's design required land on the eastern end of the club's property, including what was then holes 11, 12 and 13.

Harry Kidde, the veteran Greens Committee chairman for nearly a decade, led the Wheatley Hills team negotiating with Robert Moses, the Long Island State Parks commissioner. Kidde's team worked tirelessly and reached a very equitable deal for the club.

The state acquired 13 acres bordering on what is now Glen Cove Road. In exchange, the club received cash and a larger 21-acre plot on what is now the land north of the 13th green and 17th tee. The cash infusion allowed the club to immediately begin work on a redesign by Emmet and his partner, Alfred Tull.

Robert Moses
Chairman of the Long Island State Park Commission

Holes 10 and 18 remained intact and 17 received a new tee. The layout for the other holes changed significantly. It is noteworthy that the current 18th hole is consistent with the original Emmet design. For many years, the current ninth hole served as the finishing hole before returning to the original layout. This was also to be one of Devereaux Emmet's final projects, as he died two years later in 1934 at age 71.

12

To sum up, the sound financial condition of the club, coupled with strong leadership, allowed Wheatley Hills to emerge from the crisis with an improved and more challenging course. At the completion of the work in 1932, the total yardage increased from 6205 yards to 6505 yards. Press coverage at the time is included in the Brooklyn Eagle article on page 14.

Devereaux Emmet (right) checking on the status of course construction with his son.

BROOKLYN DAILY EAGLE, NEW YORK, SUNDAY, JANUARY 10, 1932

Wheatley Hills Links to Be Lengthened by Changes Underway

Agreement With Park Commissioner Has Been Happy Arrangement

By RALPH TROST

Those fears which so many entertained regarding Wheatley Hills' ability to carry on, what with the encroaching Northern State Parkway, the likelihood, of having to close the course, for a season or resort to the use of only nine holes and the general effect of the depression have proved totally unnecessary. Quite the contrary. Wheatley Hills seems certain to emerge from the transition and depression in better condition than ever. Certainly this will be true of the golf course. A lot of different things are contributing to Wheatley's good fortune.

In the first place Wheatley Hills' officials and Robert Moses, chairman of the Long Island State Park Commission, worked out a most equitable deal whereby the State could quickly obtain possession of the 13 odd acres bordering on Guinea Town Road, a slice right off the inward nine of the golf course. In exchange Wheatley obtained a larger, though interior, plot immediately and a sufficient cash exchange to enable it to start to work at once preparing new holes to supplant those to be taken over by the Park Commission. The remarkable open Winter has furthered the plans. Summed up the sound financial position of the club, plus the untiring services of the veteran, Harry Kidde, and the acquisition of the new property and the working cash, have arranged things so that Wheatley will not have to cease play over the full course or restrict it to nine holes. Blunt-nosed bulldozers are pushing rich top soil around furiously. Necessary tree felling has already been accomplished. Tile has been laid beneath the new green construction and given further fair breaks in the weather, Wheatley, as a full 18 holes, will be open all through next season up to about Election Day. Then it will be shut down, but hardly for more than five weeks, which will be consumed by the transferring of sod, etc., to cover those areas from which greens will have been removed.

RARE JOB IS BEING DONE

A remarkable job is being done at Wheatley. Reconstructing practically an entire nine holes without interrupting play is a neat trick comparable with the stunt accomplished by Devereaux Emmet in rebuilding the Old Country Club from a 9 to an 18-hole course, with the addition of only half a dozen acres and the utilization of all original nine greens.

No doubt about it, the ease with which Wheatley's difficulties are being ironed out has removed any doubt existing through mid-Nassau and Suffolk Counties concerning the fairness of the State Park Commission. The arrangements have been completely satisfactory to all parties. From a purely golfical point of view Wheatley, one feels, is getting a break. Circumstances necessitated the construction of the club's original second nine on a genuinely constricted plot. The holes, continually paralleling, were also of necessity rather lacking in length. It's also true that because of the continued back and forth arrangements the holes did not have a fair share of character. One brave enough to wallow through the heavy, mucky expanse of cleared and plowed land of the recently acquired acreage cannot help realizing that the new layout will not only be virtually 300 yards longer than the present, but will have holes that are different.

CHANGES AT THE FAR END

There's to be no change in the 10th. That and the 18th go unchanged. The others will be new. The greatest changes will be made on the far end. The old 11th, a 340-yard affair with no outstanding features, will be transformed into a 420-yard par 4. The par 5 being substituted for the old 12th, looms a mighty hole, what with its birch bordered, sloping, well-bunkered fairway and terraced, tree-bordered green. The new 13th, also being built on the Treadwell property will be 380 yards instead of the old distance of 302. Like the 12th, part of it runs through birches and oaks. And the hole different from the old 12th will have a slanting, well-trapped green, which will demand pitches from the long, hooking hitter and permit well-steered run-ups from the shorter drivers who will perforce have to depend upon longer clubs for approaching. Hole No. 13 in the new schemes to be a 150-yard one-shotter, played due south, which means into any or all Summer breezes. No. 15 doubles back and weaving and rolling, unwinds its 520-yard path through the value of birches and back on to the oak-clustered rise at the extreme end of the property.

THEN AND NOW

Grill Room in the 1930s

We all have heard the fairy tales that start out with "Once Upon A Time." Well, those same words can apply to the 100 years of Wheatley Hills.

HERE ARE SOME FUN FACTS AND RECOLLECTIONS

Grill Room today

A gathering around the club bar, December 26, 1945

The newly remodeled bar, 2012

The power lines have been a part of Wheatley Hills since the early 1930s.

THE CABIN

Located behind the 13th tee, it is a welcoming stop for a refreshing drink, hot dog or during the period from May of 1970 to March of 1995, the famous "Nancy Burger." A number of years ago, it was noted in the MGA Magazine that the hamburger from the cabin at Wheatley Hills was listed as the best in the metropolitan area. The term "Nancy Burger" was used by the club's members to emphasize its special quality.

Over the years, families rode out to the cabin for lunch. It was a comfortable place to enjoy eating with children.

In the 1950s, an oompah band was hired once a month to play at the cabin for the entertainment of the members. A fun night was had by all who attended.

The cabin circa 1930

KIENZLE CABIN
(at the 12th hole)
A Popular Rendezvous for Refreshments
WHEATLEY·HILLS·GOLF·CLUB

The Halfway House has been part of the landscape since the early 1930s.

The cabin as it appears today.

THE DEROSA FAMILY CHAMPS

The DeRosa family has proven that the game of golf is part of the gene pool. Both father, Gary, and son, Greg, have been champions at Wheatley Hills. Gary has won the championship twice, the first time in 1981, followed by another win in 1984; while Greg had his first win in 2008 and his second win in 2009. The unique aspect of Greg's 2009 win was that his father, Gary, was his opponent. Youth prevailed and Greg achieved his second consecutive Club Championship.

This was a wonderful sight to witness as we believe they are both fine competitors and champs at Wheatley Hills Golf Club.

The date of the first photo is September 1987 when Greg was 6 years old and the new one is September 2009 when he beat his father for the club championship.

As this 1969 menu from the club shows:

Shrimp cocktails were $1.25 and your favorite vichyssoise could be enjoyed for 50 cents a bowl. Your lobster tail would only set you back $6.75, as would a prime sirloin. Oh, yes, those were the days!

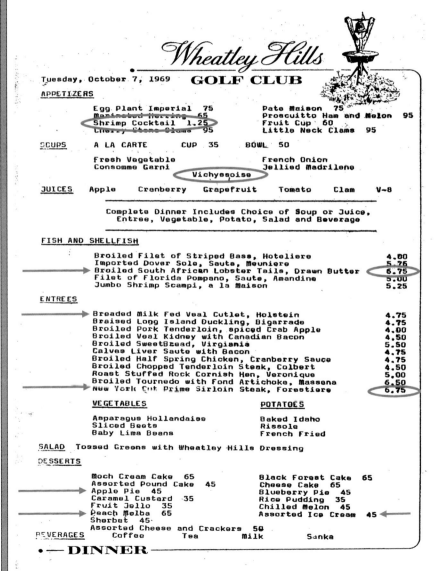

Wheatley Hills
GOLF CLUB

Tuesday, October 7, 1969

APPETIZERS

Egg Plant Imperial 75   Pate Maison 75
Marinated Herring 65   Proscuitto Ham and Melon 95
Shrimp Cocktail 1.25   Fruit Cup 60
Cherry Stone Clams 95   Little Neck Clams 95

SOUPS   A LA CARTE   CUP 35   BOWL 50

Fresh Vegetable   French Onion
Consomme Garni   Jellied Madrilene
                Vichyssoise

JUICES   Apple   Cranberry   Grapefruit   Tomato   Clam   V-8

Complete Dinner Includes Choice of Soup or Juice,
Entree, Vegetable, Potato, Salad and Beverage

FISH AND SHELLFISH

Broiled Filet of Striped Bass, Hoteliere   4.00
Imported Dover Sole, Saute, Meuniere   5.75
Broiled South African Lobster Tails, Drawn Butter 6.75
Filet of Florida Pompano, Saute, Amandine   5.00
Jumbo Shrimp Scampi, a la Maison   5.25

ENTREES

Breaded Milk Fed Veal Cutlet, Holstein   4.75
Braised Long Island Duckling, Bigarrade   4.75
Broiled Pork Tenderloin, spiced Crab Apple   4.00
Broiled Veal Kidney with Canadian Bacon   4.50
Broiled SweetBread, Virginia   5.50
Calves Liver Saute with Bacon   4.75
Broiled Half Spring Chicken, Cranberry Sauce   4.75
Broiled Chopped Tenderloin Steak, Colbert   4.50
Roast Stuffed Rock Cornish Hen, Veronique   5.00
Broiled Tournedo with Fond Artichoke, Massena   6.50
New York Cut Prime Sirloin Steak, Forestiere   6.75

VEGETABLES   **POTATOES**

Asparagus Hollandaise   Baked Idaho
Sliced Beets   Rissole
Baby Lima Beans   French Fried

SALAD   Tossed Greens with Wheatley Hills Dressing

DESSERTS

Moch Cream Cake 65   Black Forest Cake 65
Assorted Pound Cake 45   Cheese Cake 65
Apple Pie 45   Blueberry Pie 45
Caramel Custard 35   Rice Pudding 35
Fruit Jello 35   Chilled Melon 45
Peach Melba 65   Assorted Ice Cream 45
Sherbet 45
Assorted Cheese and Crackers 50

BEVERAGES   Coffee   Tea   Milk   Sanka

• — DINNER —

Wheatley Hills Golf Club

Dinner Menu

November 21, 2012

STARTERS

Beef & Mushroom Barley 5

Jumbo Shrimp Cocktail 14

Seared Ahi Tuna 14
Watercress, Sweet Peppers, Shiitake Mushrooms, Sesame Miso Dressing

Wedge Salad 8
Applewood Smoked Bacon, Cherry Tomatoes, Blue Cheese Dressing

ENTREES

Grilled T-Bone Steak & Blackened Shrimp 36
Tobacco Onion Rings, Whipped Potatoes, Asparagus
Suggested Wine Pairing: Chasing Lions Cabernet Sauvignon

Domestic Lamb Chops with Roasted Garlic 32
Rosemary Jus, Sweet Potato Puree & Sautéed Spinach
Suggested Wine: Feudi D'Albe Montepulciano

Herb Roasted Chicken 22
Broccoli Rabe & Sausage, Natural Jus
Suggested Wine Pairing: Zin 91 Zinfandel

Grilled Swordfish with Capellini Pasta 26
With Tomato, Caper & Anchovy Sauce
Suggested Wine Pairing: Kris Pinot Grigio

Penne with Beef Tips & Wild Mushrooms 18
With Red Wine Gorgonzola Sauce
Suggested Wine Pairing: Meiomi Pinot Noir

Rigatoni with Chicken, Plum Tomatoes & Broccoli 16
Basil, Garlic & Oil
Suggested Wine Pairing: Clos du Bois Chardonnay

Prime NY Sirloin Steak (14 oz.) 38 Jr. (10oz.) 27
Whipped Potatoes, Cabernet Wine Sauce, Asparagus
Suggested Wine Pairing: Simi Cabernet Sauvignon

SIMPLY GRILLED
Served with Choice of Seasonal Vegetables, Baked or Sweet Potato,
Mashed Potatoes, Sweet Potato or Regular French Fries

Breast of Chicken 21 - Salmon 22 - 8 oz. Filet Mignon 32

Setting up for a tournament 2012

Back of clubhouse in the late '40s

LEGENDS AT WHEATLEY HILLS

Wheatley Hills history is closely tied to that of three men: Willie Klein, the club's golf professional from 1926 to 1956; Jack Mallon, the golf professional from 1957 to 1973; and member Gene Francis, whose seven Long Island Amateur Championships spanned a quarter of a century.

We honor these gentlemen by telling their stories and highlighting their accomplishments. They were "Legends" and we are proud to be associated with them.

WILLIE KLEIN

It would be hard to tell the story of the club without highlighting the many successes of Willie Klein. He was born a stone's throw from Wheatley Hills and started as a caddie like most of the early professionals.

In 1926, he was teaching golf at West Palm Beach when he was talked into entering the Miami Open. He only had time to practice for one day and went out to win it with a 289, defeating Bobby Jones by 10 strokes. He repeated the feat in 1936, this time with a 272 that included an 18-hole record of 64.

Willie decided it was better to have a couple of steady jobs than to play tournament golf and so he came to Wheatley Hills as the club pro. He continued to play some tournaments, "just to let my members know I can still play golf."

He was good enough to win seven more PGA tournaments between 1926 and 1938, including the Metropolitan PGA Championship, the Mid-South Open and the New York State Open, twice. He won the Long Island Open in 1922, '23 and again in '33, while still maintaining his responsibilities at Wheatley Hills.

Willie Klein shows off his golf stance.

In 1935, he appeared at the 1935 Masters (second year) playing with the likes of Byron Nelson, Tommy Armour, Mike Turnesa, Joe Turnesa, Vic Ghezzi, Tony Manero, Bobby Cruikshank, Paul Runyan, Bobby Jones, Henry Cooper, Henry Picard and Gene Sarazen, who won the title, beating Craig Wood in a playoff.

He was the club professional from 1926 until 1956, just before his untimely death in 1957, at the age of 55. In his very first year, as the pro at Wheatley, he became famous for his round of nine holes in 29 strokes made at Shawnee.

Willie is truly a Legend and will always have a special place in the hearts of the Wheatley Hills golf family.

The 1935 Masters. Willie Klein is in the back row, fifth from the right.

JACK MALLON

GOLF SHOP
JACK MALLON, PRO.

Jack Mallon tended the Wheatley Hills Pro Shop for 16 years.

He was born in Hell's Kitchen on Manhattan's West Side, a brassie shot from Broadway's Great White Way. His family migrated to Hempstead, Long Island in 1914. Jack was introduced to golf in high school and used to walk after school to caddie and work in Jim Law's Golf Shop at Cherry Valley Club. Jack Fox, an associate of Laws, became the pro at Ekwanck Country Club, Manchester, New Hampshire and Jack joined him. He later succeeded Fox and became the youngest pro in New England. This was followed by jobs at Garden City Country Club and Cold Springs Country Club. He also spent several winters as an aide to Willie Klein at La Gorce in Miami, Florida.

Over the years, Jack proved to be one of the region's most effective golf instructors and skilled players. Four of his prized pupils were George Burns, III, PGA professional; Susan Peters Connors, 12-time Wheatley Hills Ladies Club Champion; James Dowdell, Jr., Junior Champion and five-time Club Champion; and Patricia Tiernan, four-time Wheatley Hills Ladies Club Champion.

Accomplishments during his tenure at the club were:

Winning the LIPGA 1953 and 1954 | President, Met PGA
Vice President, National PGA Organization | Met Golf Professional of the Year, 1961-1962
Met PGA Sam Snead Award (posthumously) 1974

In 1972 he was unanimously elected as an Honorary Member of Wheatley Hills Golf Club. We lost Jack Mallon in 1973, but he was again honored in 1979 when he was inducted into the PGA of America's Hall of Fame. Willie Klein and Jack Mallon formed a tandem at Wheatley that provided a positive experience for our members.

GENE FRANCIS

The Ike Tournament, named in honor of President Dwight D. Eisenhower, who was a keen amateur golfer, is an annual amateur MGA golf championship.

This prestigious trophy was captured by Gene Francis, our nine-time Club Champion, in 1971. At the time of this event, Francis was in the throes of a spring slump. Suddenly he took fire in the Ike, defeating a formidable field from every private and public club of Westchester, New Jersey, southwest Connecticut and Long Island. Gene won with rounds of 72-72-74=218. Gene birdied holes 5, 6, 7 and 9 in the final.

Comedian Bob Hope, a close friend of the late president, who was active in golf's tribute to Ike, made the presentation of the trophy to Gene at the end of the 54-hole competition.

Gene was a three-time All-American while at Purdue University and received this honor in 1958, 1959 and 1960. He was also the last Purdue golfer to be a medalist at the NCAA championships, when he topped the field in 1960.

Bob Hope presenting the Eisenhower trophy to Gene Francis.

In addition to his club championships, Gene Francis dominated the Long Island Golf Association Amateur Championship. He won seven times, finished second four times, and was the medalist on four occasions. His wins were in 1963, 1969, 1973, 1976, 1977, 1978 and again in 1988. He won the Northeast Amateur Invitational Golf Tournament in 1963, played at Wannamoisett Country Club. This prestigious championship is considered to be the "Masters of Amateur Golf."

Gene Francis playing while a student at Purdue.

Gene was a superb sand player.

Gene also was the medalist at the Long Island Golf Association Richardson Cup in 1963. He won the Northeast Amateur Anderson Memorial Championship at Winged Foot in 1967 and during his career, he played in the prestigious Masters at Augusta National.

Many of the current members knew and played with Gene. The experience was always a wonderful after-golf topic of conversation. He was a superb amateur. His untimely passing in 2006 at age 68 saddened us all, but he left us with a treasure trove of golf memories.

WHEATLEY HILLS PROFESSIONALS - 1913-2013

Most golf clubs would be fortunate to state they have had a club professional that had national recognition. At Wheatley Hills, we can name several who hold that distinction.

Starting with our first club pro in 1913, we have had some of the best overall golfers in the game.

1913-1914

BILL KANAY

Bill was not only our first club professional, but he was one of the finest golfers on Long Island at that time. We were pleased he wanted to join the new fledgling group and take the lead in getting Wheatley Hills off to a grand start.

1915-1918

E.H. WEST

As fine a job as Bill Kanay did in getting us off to a great start, E.H. West did in fine-tuning the elements needed to make Wheatley Hills a golf destination for early Long Island golfers. He played with many of the great golfers of his time and just like Bill Kanay, gave us a foundation that has done well by us for these 100 years.

1919-1925

JAMES CROSSAN

A 1922 New York Times headline tells the story of Jim Crossan, while he was the pro at Wheatley and still playing on the golf circuit. It read:

CROSSAN'S 74 BEST PRO SCORE AT LIDO

Wheatley Hills Player Leads Field in First Round of Met Open. Jim Barnes has a 78 and Sarazen an 84. "James Crossan, golf professional at the Wheatley Hills Club, is looking over his shoulder at the rest of the 130-odd players who started out today on their first round for the metropolitan open championship at the Lido Country Club."

1925-1956

WILLIE KLEIN

It would be hard to tell the story of Wheatley Hills without highlighting the many successes of Willie Klein. He was born in 1902, in New Hyde Park.

Early in his career he was noted as a free swinger who hit the ball "a mile," however, not always in the right direction.

As he learned to control the ball flight and develop his overall golf skills, his career and his success as a pro moved in a positive direction.

Klein learned golf first as a caddie, then as caddie master, under Frank Bellwood at Garden City Golf Club. He came to Wheatley Hills in October of 1925 and was our pro through 1956.

1957-1973

JACK MALLON

The Wheatley Hills Pro Shop was tended for 16 years following Klein by Jack Mallon. Jack was recognized as one of the leading players and instructors in the region. His standing as a professional was recognized by his selection as:

President, Met PGA
Vice President, National PGA Organization
Met PGA Golf Professional of the Year
Met PGA Sam Snead Award (posthumously)

Jack was further honored when the Met PGA named a Pro-Am tournament in his honor.

1974-1987

MICHAEL MALLON

Mike Mallon had spent a couple of years on tour before coming back to the club after his father's death. His goal has always been to make the game of golf enjoyable for the average player.

After leaving Wheatley Hills, he became involved with young golfers and for the past several years in Florida, he has been teaching golf to juniors. In 2005, he won the National Award from the PGA President's Council, on Growing the Game.

1987-1997

MIKE REYNOLDS

Mike Reynolds came to us from Palm Beach area clubs. He split his time being director of golf operations at the Loxahatchee Club and the Jack Nicklaus Club Management Team. He was also the head professional at PGA National Golf Club. He shared his talent with our membership for 11 years before heading to the Ibis Golf & Country Club as its director of operations.

1998-2002

MIKE GILMORE

Mike Gilmore is a golfer's golfer. He not only could teach the membership at Wheatley Hills, but he was also out winning championships. He won the 2000 Metropolitan and in 2002 was the Metropolitan PGA Player of the Year. In addition, Mike has played in the US Open and in the PGA Championship.

While at Wheatley Hills, he and our Board president, Jim Anziano, managed to win a tournament or two, including capturing first place in the Pro/President Tournament held at Pine Hollow Country Club, in East Norwich.

He left Wheatley Hills to be the pro at Piping Rock and subsequently became head pro at Winged Foot in 2009.

2003-2009

DOUG MAUCH

Doug came to us after being head pro at Tradition, Arnold Palmer's West Coast base. He was also assistant pro at Augusta National, Ardsley and Maidstone. While at Wheatley Hills he pioneered popular clinics for all members to sharpen their playing skills. Doug is the grandson of the late Gus Mauch, the longtime trainer of the New York Yankees and the New York Mets.

2010 -

JAMIE KILMER

Professional at Wheatley Hills since 2010, Jamie began learning the intricate details of pro shop responsibilities at a young pre-college age at Braelinn Golf Club in Peachtree City, Georgia. He has worked as an assistant pro at Apawamis, Stanwich and Meadow Brook Club for a total of 12 years. He was at Meadow Brook when he was tapped for Wheatley, which he will happily tell you "it was my dream come true." The people here love him, his wife, Jennifer, and new son, Luke. We are glad to have him as a part of the Wheatley Hills tradition of dedicated professionals.

CLUB CHAMPIONS HONOR ROLL

MEN'S CHAMPIONS

1914-1915	RICHARD DOWNING, JR.
1916-1917	L.E.K. WHITE
1918-1919	J.E. BAYNE, JR.
1920	D. LORD
1921	RICHARD DOWNING, JR.
1922	F.T. HAYES
1923	RICHARD DOWNING, JR.
1924	R.A. LATIMER
1925	ANDREW N. BURKHARD
1926	E.A. GUNTHER
1927	ANDREW N. BURKHARD
1928	R.D. WRIGLEY, JR.
1929-1933	ANDREW N. BURKHARD
1934-1935	DR. CHARLES J. ROBINSON
1936	CHARLES TRUNZ
1937	DR. CHARLES J. ROBINSON
1938	CHARLES TRUNZ
1939	DR. CHARLES J. ROBINSON
1940	C.A. DURAND, JR.
1941-1942	ROBERT B. ODOM
1943-1945	DR. CHARLES J. ROBINSON

1946	JAMES A. CULLEN
1947	DR. CHARLES J. ROBINSON
1948	J. COLLIER WEEKS
1949	JAMES A. CULLEN
1950-1951	FRED HEAD, JR.
1952	JAMES A. CULLEN
1953	FRED HEAD, JR.
1954	DR. S.J. ANZIANO
1955	FRED HEAD, JR.
1956-1960	DR. S.J. ANZIANO
1961-1966	GENE C. FRANCIS
1967	LOUIS FURTHNER
1968	RICHARD FRAME
1969	JOHN DESIDERIO
1970-1971	GENE C. FRANCIS
1972-1973	GEORGE BURNS, III
1974	FRANK J. FARUOLO, III
1975	RICHARD HANINGTON
1976	FRANK J. FARUOLO, III
1977	JAMES E. DOWDELL, JR.
1978	GENE C. FRANCIS

MEN'S CHAMPIONS

Year	Champion		Year	Champion
1979	JAMES E. DOWDELL, JR.		1995	RICHARD HANINGTON
1980	RICHARD HANINGTON		1996-1997	ALAN SPECHT
1981	GARY DeROSA		1998	ROBERT NAVESKY
1982	MAL GALLETTA		1999	ALAN SPECHT
1983	ROBERT NAVESKY		2000	PETER GANLEY
1984	GARY DeROSA		2001	ALAN SPECHT
1985	LON WANSER		2002	RICHARD HANINGTON
1986	ROBERT NAVESKY		2003	ALAN SPECHT
1987	JOHN E. WILSON, JR.		2004-2005	PETER GANLEY
1988-1989	JAMES E. DOWDELL, JR.		2006	BRIAN McCARDLE
1990	ROBERT SHIELDS		2007	ALAN SPECHT
1991-1992	JOHN E. WILSON, JR.		2008-2009	GREG DeROSA
1993	LON WANSER		2010-2011	JIM MAYO
1994	JAMES E. DOWDELL, JR.		2012	PETER GANLEY

In 100 years of existence, we have had members who have won multiple times. We believe the achievement should be acknowledged as we name the "Club Champions Honor Roll."

Those members who have captured four or more wins have been so designated for they displayed a vigor and spirit in their play and we honor them for their accomplishment.

RICHARD DOWNING, JR.

1914 - 1915 - 1921 - 1923

The tradition of the club championship started immediately in 1914. Mr. Downing was our first and second-time winner and then came back to claim the championship again in 1921 and '23.

ANDREW N. BURKHARD

1925 - 1927 - 1929 - 1930 - 1931 - 1932 - 1933

Mr. Burkhard was not only the winner in 1925, but continued to win again in 1927 and in 1929. He then went on to successfully defend his title each of the next four years. He was the most dominant player in the late 1920s and early 1930s.

DR. CHARLES J. ROBINSON

1934 - 1935 - 1937 - 1939 - 1943 - 1944 - 1945 - 1947

Doc held the club championship eight times. In the summer of 1946, he also won the annual Member-Guest with Wesley Cotterell, his guest from the Cherry Valley Club. They won by one stroke. Doc Robinson served as president of the Long Island Golf Association in 1944-45.

FRED HEAD, JR.

1950 - 1951 - 1953 - 1955

Fred won the Wheatley Hills Championship consecutively in the early 1950s and then went on to gain the title two more times. In 1962, Fred won the Senior Club Championship in an exciting match against Howard Schenk that was decided on the 18th green.

DR. SAM ANZIANO

1954 - 1956 - 1957 - 1958 - 1959 - 1960

Dr. Sam was the champion at Wheatley Hills six separate times. In 1959, Jack Mallon and Dr. Sam Anziano won the Long Island Golf Association's Pro-Amateur title at the Nassau Country Club in Glen Cove with a 4-under-par 66. He also tied for first place (65) with Jack Mallon in the 1965 Long Island Golf Tournament, which was played at Wheatley Hills.

GENE FRANCIS

1961 - 1962 - 1963 - 1964 - 1965 - 1966 - 1970 - 1971 - 1978

Gene was a nine-time Club Champion. His wins spanned two decades and started in 1961. He won the Long Island Amateur Championship seven times. His first win was in 1963. He also won in 1969, 1973, 1976, 1977, 1978 and 1988.

RICHARD HANINGTON
1975 - 1980 - 1995 - 2002

Dick was a winner in four separate decades. He was a runner-up in the Long Island Amateur in 1975 and has played in both the USGA Senior Amateur and the British Senior Open Amateur. They call him the "IceMan" because he plays with no emotion. He says, "I play a shot and forget it." Good lesson to be learned from Mr. Hanington.

JAMES E. DOWDELL, JR.
1977 - 1979 - 1988 - 1989 - 1994

Jim learned to play golf at Wheatley Hills in our Junior Golf League. He won the WHGC Boys Championship in 1965. In 1975, he was runner-up in the Richardson Invitational and in 1977, he went on to finish second in the annual tournament at the Seawane Club. It was his first appearance in a major golf tournament. He won the Long Island Amateur Medal in 1988 and was Club Champion on five separate occasions at Wheatley. In addition, he won multiple Father-Son tournaments with Jim Sr.

ALAN SPECHT

1996 - 1997 - 1999 - 2001 - 2003 - 2007

Alan, following in Gene Francis' footsteps, won the Long Island Amateur Championship in 2008. Making putts in critical situations was crucial to his winning six Club Championships. Alan's friendly demeanor on and off the course makes him a pleasure to play with, regardless of one's level of skill. He can often be found fine-tuning his skills on the driving range.

PETER GANLEY

2000 - 2004 - 2005 - 2012

2012 was a great year for Peter Ganley. Peter won both the Wheatley Hills Club Championship and the Senior Championship. In addition, he and Lee Ann Lewis of Southward Ho teamed up to win the 49th MGA/WMGA mixed Pinehurst Championship at the Tuxedo Club.

WOMEN'S CHAMPIONS HONOR ROLL

Congratulations to those women members who have captured three or more championship wins.

1926	MRS. N.A. BROWN	1938	MISS GLADYS DURAND
1927	MRS. W.J. ROONEY	1939	MISS MADELINE WHITE
1928	MRS. F.T. HAYES	1940	MRS. R. STUTZMANN
1929	MRS. W.J. ROONEY	1941	MRS. R. STUTZMANN
1930	MRS. F.T. HAYES	1942-1948	MISS EVELYN ODOM
1931	H.B.W. HAFF	1949	MRS. A. HANTSCHE
1932	MRS. J.A. BURGUN	1950-1952	MISS EVELYN ODOM
1933	MRS. GEO. VIEBROCK	1953-1954	FRIEDA MEISSNER
1934	MISS M. CORROON	1955-1956	PATRICIA TIERNAN
1935	MRS. J.A. BURGUN	1957	FRIEDA MEISSNER
1936	MISS MADELINE WHITE	1958-1959	PATRICIA TIERNAN
1937	MISS MADELINE WHITE	1960	BARBARA HEVENER

They have been so designated for the Championship Honor Roll because they faced a challenging experience and each of the women champions has managed it with ease and grace.

WOMEN'S CHAMPIONS

1961	FRIEDA MEISSNER		1982-1984	NORA DOWDELL
1962-1963	GLADYS PARZINI		1985	THECLA STELLATO
1964	FRIEDA MEISSNER		1986	MARGARET FIDUCIA
1965	SUSAN V. PETERS		1987	TRUDY KLOOCK
1966	GLADYS PARZINI		1988-1989	MARILYN FRAME
1967-1969	SUSAN V. PETERS		1990-1998	TRUDY KLOOCK
1970	CHARLOTTE TRAPANI		1999-2002	PAMELA WILSON
1971-1972	SUSAN V. PETERS		2003-2004	RACHEL ZARGHAMI
1973	GLADYS PARZINI		2005-2006	LISA KENNEDY
1974	SUSAN V. PETERS		2007	NORMA ROBERTO
1975	SHARKEY TRAPANI		2008	SAMANTHA SMITH
1976-1977	SUSAN V. PETERS		2009	TRUDY KLOOCK
1978-1980	SUSAN CONNORS		2010	ROSEMARIE QUIGG
1981	TRACY HAUTH		2011-2012	SAMANTHA SMITH

MISS MADELINE WHITE | 1936 - 1937 - 1939

WHEATLEY HILLS CHAMPION THREE TIMES

Madeline was the first of over 30 Wheatley Hills women to win our Women's Golf Championship. Her wins were in 1936, 1937 and 1939. Documents show she was a finalist in the North South Women's Golf Tournament in 1942, at Pinehurst, N.C. She was also a cousin of Bob Zipse, another star player at Wheatley Hills and is most probably the daughter of our second champion, L.E.K. White.

FRIEDA MEISSNER
1953 - 1954 - 1957 - 1961 - 1964

WHEATLEY HILLS CHAMPION FIVE TIMES

She won in 1953, 1954, 1957, 1961 and again in 1964. In 1963, she won the Silver Foils Club Championship, in Pinehurst, N.C. She also won championships at two other clubs - Pomonok, eight different times and Oakland, twice.

MISS EVELYN ODOM | 1942 - 1943 - 1944 - 1945 1946 - 1947 - 1948 - 1950 - 1951 - 1952

WHEATLEY HILLS CHAMPION 10 TIMES

Evelyn was born and raised on Long Island, but because she showed promise as a young golfer, attended college at the University of Florida, to fine-tune her skills. Her first significant win was in the Florida Women Amateur Golf Championship in 1949, at the Ponte Vedra Country Club.

Her wins in New York were reported from the metropolitan area all the way to the Canadian border. Her play representing Wheatley Hills was extraordinary, winning the Club Championship consecutively from 1942 -1948 and again from 1950-1952. She won several titles in New York, including winning the first four-ball tournament held by the Women's Cross County Golf Association. She and our pro, Willie Klein, were often a duo for charity events and playing Pro-Am tournaments. Evelyn's father, Robert, was a two-time Club Champion in 1941-1942.

PATRICIA TIERNAN
1955 - 1956 - 1958 - 1959
WHEATLEY HILLS CHAMPION FOUR TIMES

Patricia was rated as the top female golfer in the Women's Long Island Golf Association in 1960. She was the Woman's Club Champion for 1955, 1956, 1958 and again in 1959.

GLADYS PARZINI
1962 - 1963 - 1966 - 1973
WHEATLEY HILLS CHAMPION FOUR TIMES

Gladys Parzini was a back-to-back winner in the 1962-63 seasons and went on to win again in 1966 and 1973.

SUSAN PETERS (CONNORS)
1965 - 1967 - 1968 - 1969 - 1971 - 1972 - 1974 - 1976 - 1977 - 1978 - 1979 - 1980

WHEATLEY HILLS CHAMPION 12 TIMES

Susan Peters was the youngest club champion at a private club in Long Island. She was the Women's Cub Champion for the first time in 1965, at the age of 15. She went on to do it 11 more times in the next 20 years.

PAM WILSON
1999 - 2000 - 2001 - 2002

WHEATLEY HILLS CHAMPION FOUR TIMES

Pam Wilson was a force to be reckoned with between 1999 and 2002. She won the championship for four consecutive years.

NORA DOWDELL
1982 - 1983 - 1984

WHEATLEY HILLS CHAMPION THREE TIMES

Nora was a complete golfer, a strong competitor and a team player. In 1976, as captain, she led the Wheatley team to victory in the Long Island Interclub League of the Women's MGA. She was also an avid and proficient bowler.

Her son, James, who started as a junior golfer, also won club championships. Mother and son both won trophies in the 1980s.

SAMANTHA SMITH
2008 - 2011 - 2012

WHEATLEY HILLS CHAMPION THREE TIMES

Samantha has been the Club Champion in 2008, 2011 and in 2012. She is a third-generation member whose family has over 40 years at Wheatley. A strong competitor and long driver with a well-balanced game, she enjoys playing from the men's tees and being competitive at that level.

TRUDY KLOOCK
1987 - 1990 - 1991 - 1992 - 1993 - 1994 - 1995 - 1996 - 1997 - 1998 - 2009

WHEATLEY HILLS CHAMPION 11 TIMES

Trudy Kloock was introduced to golf by her husband, Herb, and loved the game from the start. She won her first championship here at Wheatley Hills in 1987 and dominated the winning circle between 1989 and 1998. Her last championship win was in 2009, 22 years after her first.

THE GOLF COURSE

HOW THE COURSE EVOLVED

As we prepare to celebrate our centennial anniversary, we reflect on the many changes that have produced the golf course that we currently enjoy. In spite of all the challenges we had to overcome, Wheatley Hills has flourished and become one of the premier golf clubs on Long Island.

Once the course was rearranged in the 1930s, it stayed relatively unchanged until significant changes started taking shape again in the 1960s.

The 1960s saw the initiation of extensive tree planting on many golf courses, including Wheatley Hills. Wheatley participated in this Green Belt Movement and literally thousands of trees of various varieties surrounded the greens, tees and fairways.

Unfortunately the '70s and '80s ushered in a new movement, which rendered the tree plantings as a negative influence. The addition of greater spending on golf and golf courses, the Augusta Syndrome, the popularity of PGA events on TV and the green speed quantification brought about by the advent of the stimpmeter, combined to change the expectations for golf course conditioning. The cutting heights on greens, tees and fairways were steadily lowered to achieve the new expectations for playability. The 7-foot stimpmeter reading that was considered very appropriate in the '70s was no longer acceptable and heights of cut came from a $1/4$ inch, down to $1/10$ inch and below in many cases.

With the dramatically lower amount of leaf tissue left on the plant to perform the necessary photosynthesis, putting green turf was struggling to stay alive. The problem was clearly accentuated by all the trees now around the greens. The short height of the cut and the blocked sunlight was a toxic combination for greens turf and also tees and fairways, in many cases. Wheatley, as well as most other courses, entered a new stage that focused heavily on tree removal.

The new millennium brought many changes to our golf course. We commissioned the golf course architectural firm of Hurdzan and Fry to renovate the course, with respect to the original Devereaux Emmet design. Coincidentally at about the same time, we hired Steve Rabideau, a golf course superintendent with excellent credentials and experience. He instituted a successful tree removal plan that became the driving force in our maintenance program. With the new design features and the necessary tree removal, playing conditions improved immediately. Now there is great flexibility in tee location, the open vistas give a more majestic feel and the bunkering is beautiful and strategically challenging. We believe that if Devereaux Emmet came by today, he would say two things. "Boy do I feel old" and "This place looks wonderful."

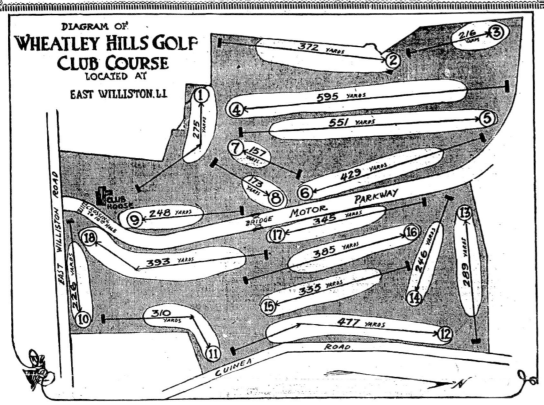

Where New York Plays Its Golf

DIAGRAM OF
WHEATLEY HILLS GOLF
CLUB COURSE
LOCATED AT
EAST WILLISTON. L.I.

Hole	Yards	Par
1	275	4
2	372	4
3	216	4
4	595	5
5	551	5
6	429	5
7	157	3
8	173	3
9	248	4
10	226	4
11	310	4
12	477	5
13	289	4
14	246	4
15	335	4
16	385	4
17	345	4
18	393	4

DIAGRAM ABOVE AND THIS STORY WERE PUBLISHED IN THE EVENING TELEGRAM, MARCH 20, 1915.

Wheatley Hills is among the most recent of golf courses in the metropolitan district, but its development has been along scientific lines, and it holds forth great promise to golfers.

Each hole has been the subject of careful study. Many of them have been modeled in a general way after the style of feature holes on some of the better known courses with a view of having Wheatley Hills stand as a composite reproduction of the best qualities of these links.

The course is 6022 yards in length and has a par of 74. The longest hole is the fourth, 505 yards and the shortest, the seventh, at 157 yards.

The article continued on to state that the new 18-hole course exemplifies the demand for golf courses on Long Island, where the presence of so many suburban homes makes golf playing the ideal sport for the man of business.

THE COURSE AFTER THE RECONSTRUCTION IN 1932

The Evening Telegram, March 20, 1915 article continued on to state that the Wheatley Hills Golf Club's construction work is moving ahead swiftly along the plans illustrated in the diagram to the right. Only the holes as they will be played after construction are shown. Holes No. 10, 17 and 18, as shown, are practically identical with the holes now being played. All other present holes will be changed to conform with the illustrated arrangement, giving the club not only a far longer but a far stronger inward nine for play in the 1933 season.

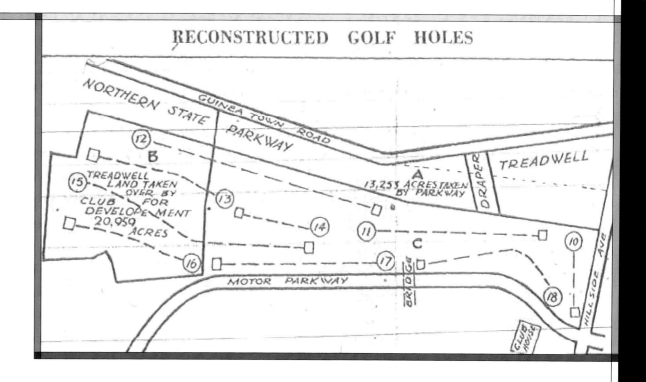

RECONSTRUCTED GOLF HOLES

OUR COURSE TODAY

#1 PAR 4

Blue: 339 yds. HDCP: 16 | White: 322 yds. HDCP: 14

At first glance this short par 4 seems an easy birdie hole, but out of bounds lurks left and trees on the right will block any approach from that side. From the tee, the fairway climbs a steep hill, with one bunker short to the right and one bunker further down the fairway on the left. The putting surface has subtle breaks with the toughest pin up front. A miss over this green becomes a very difficult up and down.

#2 PAR 4

Blue: 367 yds. HDCP: 12 | White: 355 yds. HDCP: 8

Based upon USGA research, the second hole plays more difficult for the higher HDCP player. The fairway bunker is 220 yards to carry with out of bounds left. The steep hill requires an extra club for the approach. In the face of the hill, there is an original Devereaux Emmet bunker on the left, 25 yards from the green. Another bunker lies short of the green right, which catches punch shots into the green from the right side. The perimeter of the green is unprotected and the putting surface breaks sharply down from the right rear to the left front with the toughest pin positions on the right.

#3 PAR 3

Blue: 204 yds. HDCP: 8 | White: 181 yds. HDCP: 10

The par-3 third plays from an elevated tee over a gully to a rising fairway that falls into the green. The hole is bunkered well out front on the left, then at green side on both sides, and at the rear. The green runs away, then slopes up at the rear. This hole is always a difficult par, and arguably the toughest par 3 on the course.

#4 PAR 5

Blue: 570 yds. HDCP: 6 | White: 535 yds. HDCP: 4

The tee shot on this par-5 fourth hole plays to a gently rising fairway, with bunkers left and right that come into play for the longer hitter. For the second shot, bunkers lie left, just short of the landing area that rises to a crest 120 yards from home. The real challenge to this hole is the putting surface. This green is unprotected, but falls sharply from the left rear. Any shot placed above the hole will result in a lightning fast putt.

#5 PAR 5

Blue: 534 yds. HDCP: 14 | White: 502 yds. HDCP: 16

The fifth, a second consecutive par 5, plays from an elevated tee to a narrow, rolling fairway protected by fescue on the right and tall trees on the left. The player trying to get home in two must contend with difficult cross bunkers 90 yards in front of the green, not to mention bunkers surrounding the green left, right and behind. The putting surface breaks down from a modest upper tier at the right rear.

#6 PAR 3

Blue: 214 yds. HDCP: 10 | White: 185 yds. HDCP: 12

The par-3 sixth plays to a relatively level green that is bunkered twice right and twice left. From the elevated championship tee, the angle is sharper, bringing the left front bunker more into the line of play.

#7 PAR 5

Blue: 539 yds. HDCP: 2 | White: 504 yds. HDCP: 2

The par-5 seventh doglegs right, with penalizing fescue on that side, as well as bunkers left and right, calling for a drive to the left of the center. The fairway rolls slightly downhill through the turn, then abruptly uphill over the last 100 yards, requiring an extra club for the approach. The green is bunkered about 50 yards out front on either side. The putting surface breaks quickly from the right front to the left rear.

#8 PAR 3

Blue: 153 yds. HDCP: 18 | White: 143 yds. HDCP: 18

The short par-3 eighth plays downhill from an elevated tee to a green bunkered twice to the left, and twice to the right. The putting surface tilts severely from back to front.

#9 PAR 4

Blue: 426 yds. HDCP: 4 | White: 374 yds. HDCP: 6

The par-4 ninth fairway is bunkered on both sides about 150 yards from the green, with out of bounds along the right side. The approach shot to this elevated green plays surprisingly long, so consider an extra club, but you do not want to be long. The putting surface, with a bunker guarding both the right front and left front of the green, tilts severely from back to front.

#10 PAR 3

Blue: 207 yds. HDCP: 7 | White: 174 yds. HDCP: 13

The par-3 10th plays from a slightly elevated tee to a severe back-to-front green. Two bunkers sit out front, leaving an entrance of just 15 yards between them, and bunkers flank the sides as well. The putting surface also features two short ridges extending from near the center of the green toward the back corners.

#11 PAR 4

Blue: 462 yds. HDCP: 1 | White: 428 yds. HDCP: 1

The triple-bunkered par-4 11th hole is the strongest of Wheatley Hills' 10 par 4s. A precise tee shot is required here, with out of bounds right, trees right and left, and bunkers on the right side flanking the drive zone 200 yards from the green. The hole curves slightly to the right in the landing area, then rolls to an elevated green with a deep bunker at the right front that comes into play. A wide back-to-front spine separates the right and left sides of the putting surface.

#12 PAR 5

Blue: 533 yds. HDCP: 9 | White: 507 yds. HDCP: 7

The scenic par-5 12th hole is narrowed by trees and out of bounds to the right. The hole rises to the crest of a ridge 200 yards from the green, which is flanked by deep bunkers, one left and two right. The putting surface features an upper tier across the back and around to the right front.

#13 PAR 4

Blue: 329 yds. HDCP: 13 | White: 315 yds. HDCP: 11

The short par-4 13th plays from a slightly elevated tee down a narrow rolling fairway that is flanked by bunkers within the final 100 yards. The elongated, elevated green requires an extra club on the approach and is heavily bunkered left, right and behind the green. The putting surface tilts sharply back to front.

#14 PAR 3

Blue: 186 yds. HDCP: 15 | White: 156 yds. HDCP: 17

The par-3 14th plays to a relatively wide target that is protected by three bunkers, one in front, one left and one right. A high, soft shot is required to hold this green. The putting surface falls slightly back to front.

#15 PAR 5

Blue: 618 yds. HDCP: 3 | White: 577 yds. HDCP: 3

The par-5 15th is exceptionally long, uphill and is the strongest of Wheatley Hills' five par 5s. A tall tree stands 400 yards out on the right, calling for a drive to the left center. The hole rises, falls, then rises again over its last 200 yards, playing to a relatively small green bunkered left and twice right.

#16 PAR 4

Blue: 343 yds. HDCP: 17 | White: 331 yds. HDCP: 15

The par-4 16th plays down into a valley off the tee, with a bunker on the right between 80 and 100 yards from home. The table-top green is protected across the front left by a large bunker. A second bunker on the right side and trees behind the steeply back-to-front putting green add an additional challenge.

#17 PAR 4

Blue: 406 yds. HDCP: 11 | White: 393 yds. HDCP: 9

The par-4 17th gives a more open appearance, with a lone bunker short of the drive zone to the right. The fairway is divided about 90 yards from home by a small patch of rough that includes an original Devereaux Emmet "Principal's Nose" bunker. The back-to-front green is bunkered left and twice right.

#18 PAR 4

Blue: 437 yds. HDCP: 5 | White: 383 yds. HDCP: 5

This par-4 Wheatley Hills' home fairway turns to the right, with trees close by on that side. The fairway falls into a swale before rising to the green. The putting surface, one of the course's toughest, is bracketed by bunkers front left and behind, and breaks sharply from the right rear down to the left front and also over a small ridge toward the left side.

This is a photo of the putting green in the 1940s.

Note the bell was still in the center of the putting green.

WHEATLEY HILLS CELEBRITY CONNECTIONS

GENE SARAZEN

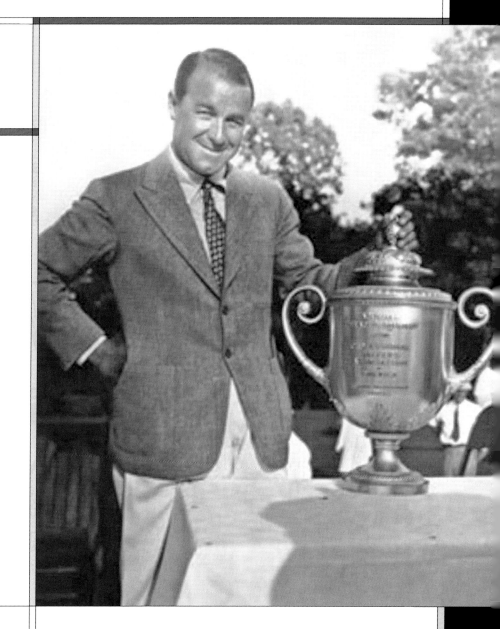

Gene Sarazen was a friend and competitor of Willie Klein. Competition was fierce and they often switched between coming in first and second in local tournaments.

Both men won the Metropolitan PGA and the Long Island Open more than once as they played the golf circuit together in the '20s and '30s.

Sarazen and Klein both played in the Masters in 1935. Gene won in a playoff with Craig Wood. Willie did well in the first round, but was not in the competition after that.

Gene was eventually the pro at Fresh Meadows while Willie was pro at Wheatley Hills. They would show up at each other's links to play a round of golf with members of both Long Island clubs.

GEORGE BURNS, III

Often we tend to overlook the fact that we have "stars" in our midst. We had one in George Burns, III. He was a member and a two-time champion here at Wheatley Hills. He won several prestigious amateur championships, including the 1972 Metropolitan Amateur, Monroe Invitational and the Long Island Amateur. In 1973, he won the Canadian Amateur Championship and in '74, he won the Azalea Invitational, Porter Cup, North and South Amateur, NYS Amateur and the Ike Championship.

As a professional, he won four times on the PGA Tour, three times on the European Tour and won three other tournaments during his professional career.

SAM SNEAD

Sam Snead played at Wheatley with member Burkly Andrews. Mr. Andrews was owner of the "White Fortress," a chain of hamburger restaurants similar to "White Castle."

At the time of Snead's visit to Wheatley Hills, he and Burkly were discussing a venture to build and operate a driving range together.

JOE NAMATH

Gene Francis and Joe Namath take a moment for a photo with Wheatley members Morton Bouchard and Kevin Quigley and John O'Neill from Garden City Golf Club.

John O'Neill, Kevin Quigley, Joe Namath,
Mort Bouchard and Gene Francis.

MIKE DITKA

In the recent past, Mike Ditka, coach of the Chicago Bears, the 1986 Super Bowl Champions, played golf at Wheatley with his friend and member Stan Mackney.

Stan says, "Mike had a single-digit handicap, could hit the ball a long way and although competitive, was fun to play with."

KEEGAN BRADLEY

Keegan Bradley autographs a hat for Kyle McGorty during the Zurich Invitational Golf Tournament, August 2012, at Wheatley Hills.

Keegan Bradley started his golfing career at Wheatley Hills while playing for the St. John's University golf team. Upon turning pro, Keegan was supported by a group of Wheatley members, led by Dr. Glenn Muraca. Keegan is now an honorary member of the club.

Keegan exploded on the PGA TOUR scene in 2011, winning the Byron Nelson, PGA Championship, PGA Grand Slam of Golf and capturing Tour Rookie of the Year Award. In 2012, he won the WGC Bridgestone Invitational and starred in his Ryder Cup debut. He finished 2012 as 13th in the world rankings.

We were fortunate enough to have him join fellow pro, Justin Rose, to play a tournament at Wheatley Hills, sponsored by Zurich Insurance Company.

Keegan Bradley with his foursome, John Treiber, Jim Harrison, Keegan, in center, Dick Kearns and Jim D'Addario, at the Zurich Invitational Tournament.

JUSTIN ROSE

Justin finished 2012 as number four in the world rankings. His biggest win to date, the 2012 WGC Cadillac Championship, made Justin just one of three British players to win four or more events on the PGA TOUR. His 3 points in the Ryder Cup at Medinah included an impressive singles win over Phil Mickelson.

Justin got the attention of the golf world when he finished fourth in the 1998 Open Championship at Royal Birkdale as a 17-year-old amateur.

Following the Zurich customer outing, Keegan and Justin prepare for the three-hole charity exhibition on par-5 holes 4, 5 and 7. Justin drilled his birdie putt on number 7 to win by one stroke.

The golfers ready themselves to play the Zurich Invitational, held at Wheatley Hills, August 2012.

JACK NICHOLSON

Vincent Massina, Jim D'Addario, Peter Ganley, Jack Nicholson and Jeff Mulhall, playing the Sherwood Country Club fundraiser.

WHEATLEY FOURSOME WINS UCLA GOLF TOURNAMENT TO BENEFIT PEDIATRIC KIDNEY RESEARCH

May 18, 1998 Sherwood Country Club, Westlake, California – Vincent C. Massina, Jim D'Addario, Jeff Mulhall and Peter Ganley playing with Academy Award-winning actor Jack Nicholson, tied for first low gross with an impressive 13 under par. All team members participated in the success, with Nicholson sinking five long putts for birdie or eagle. Team Nicholson broke the three-way tie on the second hole of a sudden death playoff, after Jack himself drained another 25-footer for birdie, proclaiming to the more than 100 spectators, "Baby, that's as good as it gets."

MULTIGENERATIONAL WHEATLEY HILLS FAMILIES

Families have played an important role in the history and development of Wheatley Hills over the past 100 years. Several families have multigenerational continuous membership in excess of 50 years.

Their ongoing support and dedication to the prosperity of the club has created a solid foundation for the continued steadfast growth at Wheatley Hills.

Al Schaeffner

Al Schaeffner joined the club in 1935 and served as president in 1946. His son-in-law, Warren Nolan, joined in 1951, served on the Board of Governors for three terms and was president in 1979. Warren has been active in many Board committees in his 61 years of membership. The Schaeffner-Nolan families have a 78-year history at Wheatley Hills.

John Treiber

The Treiber family traces its Wheatley history back 77 years to John Treiber's membership in 1936. Over the years, 14 different Treiber family members have belonged to the club, covering three generations. John's son, Howard Treiber, served as a three-term club president in 1967-69 and Howard's son John was president in 1992 during his three terms on the Board. John's wife, Carol Ann, is active with the Wheatley women's group and his brothers Bruce and Scott have been members for many years. The family has sponsored the Treiber Memorial Tournament since 1981, one of the long-running Met PGA tournaments. The Treiber family involvement and leadership, both on and off the course, continue to have a lasting impact on our club.

Brothers Louis and Dr. Sam Anziano joined Wheatley Hills in 1942 and 1943, respectively, and both served on the Board of Governors. Dr. Sam was a six-time Club Champion in 1954 and 1956-60 and represented the club in many of the Bermuda Tournaments in the 1950s.

Dr. Sam Anziano

His sons Sam Jr. and Jim became second-generation members, continuing a 71-year tradition. Jim served two terms on the Board of Governors and was club president in 1988. His wife, Anita, is also active in the women's group.

John Adikes

John Adikes joined the club in 1946, followed by his son, Park, in 1956. John's brother Larry was also a member for many years. Both John and Park served on the Board of Governors and were active on Board committees. Park's wife, Maryedith, joined as an associate member in 1970.

Their daughter, Patricia Hill, is a member, along with her son Frank Hill, continuing the four generations of Adikes family membership at Wheatley Hills during the last 67 years.

Vincent "Pop" Massina

Vincent F. Massina joined Wheatley Hills in 1950, beginning a three-generation, 63-year family history. His sons Vincent M., Robert and Richard, as well as his daughter Kate and son-in-law, John Wilson, were active members. Vincent M. served as club president in 1977 and John in 1982. Robert served on the Board of Governors as well. The third generation is well represented by Vincent C. Massina, who served as two-term club president in 1999-2000. John Wilson, Jr. was a two-time Club Champion in 1991-2 and his wife, Pam, won the Wheatley Hills Women's Championship in 1999. Richard Jr., was also one of the 10 family members over the years. The Massina and Wilson families have set the standard for golf excellence and stewardship in their long history at Wheatley Hills.

Alfred J. Schrafel, Sr.

Alfred J. Schrafel, Sr. joined the club in 1951, beginning four generations of membership involving 10 family members over the years. The Schrafels have a great history of competitive golf and active service at Wheatley Hills. Al Jr. served as president in 1978 and has been active in several committees over his five terms on the Board. His sons Robert, Richard and Thomas comprise the third generation. Richard's son Andrew is a junior member, extending the 62-year history to a fourth generation. Margaret, Barbara and Jane Schrafel represent three generations of membership in the Wheatley women's group.

Leo McGinity

Leo McGinity joined in 1951, along with his close friend, Warren Nolan. Leo was the Membership Committee chair during his two terms on the Board of Governors. His sons Leo Jr. and C.V. continue the family's 62-year active association. C.V. also served on the Board and was club president in 2010-11. The McGinitys have a great record of leadership and competitive golf at Wheatley Hills.

Jim Dowdell, Sr.

Jim Dowdell, Sr. joined the club in 1958. Jim's wife, Nora, was a three-time Ladies Champion (1982-84) and son Jim Jr. was the Club Champion five times (1977,'79, '88-9, '94) and his son Jesse has been a member for many years.

In addition to their success on the golf course, Nora and Jim were champion bowlers in the mixed league days of the '60s and '70s.

William Mulhall

The Mulhall family dates back to 1951, when Bill joined the club, followed by his wife, Elise, in 1956. Their son Jeff joined as a junior member in 1973 and Jeff's daughter Meaghan is a junior member, representing the third generation. The Mulhalls have spent many special family moments together in their 62 years at Wheatley Hills.

Vincent M. Kearns

Vincent M. Kearns joined in 1959, starting a four-generation and 54-year tradition for the Kearns family. Both Vincent and son Dick served terms as treasurer on the Board of Governors and Dick served also as Membership Committee chairman. Vincent E. Kearns was also a member for many years and also served on the Board as secretary. Dick's son Brian and son-in-law Bill Urkiel are regular members and Bill's son Ryan Urkiel is a fourth-generation junior member. The Kearns ladies have been well represented over the years through Dick's mom, Betty, and his wife, Mo, who served as the women's chairlady. Mo's dad and Bill's grandfather were caddies together at Wheatley Hills in the 1930s.

Pop Urkiel's actual
caddie pin from the 1930s

Jim Needham

The Needham family's 52-year association started with Jim in 1961, followed by his brother John in 1969. Jim served on the Board and also as treasurer.

President Richard M. Nixon appointed Jim as SEC commissioner in 1969 and in 1972, he became the first full-time chairman of the New York Stock Exchange. In 1985, President Ronald Reagan appointed Jim the U.S. ambassador to the International Exposition in Japan.

John has been a very effective Board and committee contributor, serving as club president in 1981 and in 1994. John's son-in-law, Dick Taylor, was a member of the Board and also served as secretary during his two terms. His sons, Keith and Alex, were junior members.

John's wife, Eileen, served as chairlady of Wheatley's Woman's Golf Association in 1999 and 2000.

Cal Rafuse

Cal Rafuse joined in 1962 and his wife, Pinky, also became an associate member. They were active in golf and social activities at Wheatley for many years and Cal served on the Board of Governors as vice president and Greens and House Maintenance Committee chairman. He is responsible for the present-day design of the cabin.

Andrew joined as a junior member in 1967 and he continues the family 51-year tradition with the club. He served as president and chairman of the Greens and Membership Committees during his three terms on the Board of Governors. Andrew's late wife, Joanne, was active in the women's association and his sister Carole was a junior member.

The Mormando family traces its 50-year relationship to Nick's joining in 1963, followed later by his brother Dusty, who was a member for many years. Serving on the Board of Governors, Nick was House Committee chairman, sharing his many years of experience in the restaurant business. He also cheered on the two bowling leagues

Nick Mormando

in the 1960s and '70s as an ambassador of his beloved sport. Nick's son Frank and grandson Nicholas F. represent the second and third generation of Wheatley memories for the Mormando family.

Other long-standing families are the Courtneys with 47 years and three generations, the Smiths with 40 years of membership and three generations, the Arsenaults with 28 years and three generations, the Bouchard family with 20 years and three generations and the Petruzillo family with 19 years and three generations.

In addition to families, we have a number of long-standing members of 45 or more years: Stan (Sonny) Mackney (63), Bud Munro (55), Jim Bernhart (54), Al Santos (50), Bob Roberto (49) and Dr. Joe Troisi (47).

Nancy Evans joined as a junior member in 1957. Her father, Silyn, joined in 1951 and both her mother, Alberta, and sister, Margretta, were associate members.

We would also like to recognize the contributions of the McDermott, Peters, Frame, Caprise, Meyer, Fiducia, Faruolo and Valentine families.

The club thanks all these families and individuals for their loyal membership, willingness to serve and, importantly, for the leadership they have provided Wheatley Hills over many years.

THE BELL

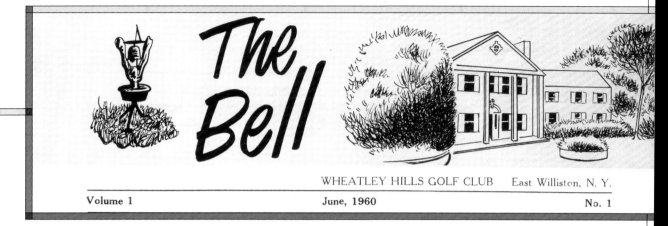

The Bell

WHEATLEY HILLS GOLF CLUB   East Williston, N. Y.

Volume 1   June, 1960   No. 1

Invariably, when a club decides to issue a publication, the problem of selecting a name develops into a wild guessing game, bordering on confusion. But not so when the enthusiastic group at Wheatley Hills made the name selection... and emerged with the name of THE BELL.

Anybody who has been around our grounds for a brief period has been fascinated by the ancient, weather-beaten bell that is surrounded by our practice putting green.

The Bell has weathered the storms of many generations. It is our fervent hope to have THE BELL, now in its first issue, survive the years and prove enjoyable to our members and their offspring.

Excerpt from The Bell, Vol. 1, No. 1, June 1960

In June 1960, Wheatley Hills president, Jim Walsh, introduced The Bell, a bulletin intended to improve communications throughout the year with a membership that totaled over 530 at the time. Long before the advent of e-mail and social media, The Bell served as the primary source of sharing news with the membership, reporting results of golf competitions, social activities and family milestones.

From the first issue in June 1960, until May 1982, the Bell editor was John Brennan, who served for many years as the golf writer for the Long Island Press. The Bell was published monthly, capturing the spirit and culture of the club life on and off the course.

Competitive golf has been synonymous with Wheatley Hills since its early years and continues today. The Bell contains many interesting stories about club tournaments and Wheatley Hills teams that played competitively in the LI area. For almost 20 years, a Wheatley team also competed annually in the Goodwill Bermuda Pro-Am Tournament, winning the cup in 1961.

The club had a very active social life in those days, including dancing every Saturday night. The July 1963 Bell reported "Saturday night dancing on the terrace has proven so popular that Bob Lahey (entertainment chairman) has ordered the time for dancing extended from 2 to 3 a.m.!" Bowling was very popular, with a Monday night mixed league for husbands and wives and a Friday morning ladies league, providing fun and friendly competition.

Also illustrating the impact of families in those years, The Bell reported that the 1963 children's Christmas party was attended by 356 kids and 235 adults, followed by 120 diners that evening.

Wheatley Hills, clipping par by 23 strokes, then winning a playoff, carried the Bermuda Trophy. Sir Julian Gascoigne, governor of Bermuda, stands w our winning team at the award ceremonies. L. to r., are Father Bill Gov Dr. Sam Anziano, Sir Julian, Jack Mallon and Dr. Rocco Zaino.

Bermuda Goodwill Cup Won After Playoff

The British colony of Bermuda will never forget the scintillating victory our Wheatley Hills team in the ninth annual Goodwill tournament that attrac a field of 86 clubs. After posting a net of 184, 23 less than par for three cou of the tight, little isle, our team tied with Riviera of Coral Gables, necessita a playoff.

SPRING 1998
CLUB NEWS
Wheatley Hills Golf Club
East Williston, NY

The format of The Bell remained consistent for 22 years and much of the club's rich history is well preserved in these volumes.

In the summer of 1982, The Bell became an internally produced newsletter with less frequent publication throughout the next 16 years. In 1998, then-President Jim Anziano asked Perry Vascellaro to revitalize The Bell with the idea of having three to four editions per year. Jim remembered growing up reading the news about Wheatley Hills in The Bell and understood the value it could bring to the membership culture. Perry enthusiastically took on the editor task with the able assistance of his wife, Denise.

The Millennium 2000 Bell edition was the most comprehensive historical document on Wheatley Hills ever prepared and published, thanks to the efforts of Perry, Denise, Janet D'Addario and then-manager, Toni DeMay. Copies of The Bell are available to review for members who would like to relive or learn about the history and personality of Wheatley Hills over the past 50 years.

A regular column entitled "From Tee to Green" captured interesting golf updates and accomplishments while "The 19th Hole" column was dedicated to sharing personal news about members, their families, travels and special occasions, similar to the "Did You Know" column of later years.

The following pages relive some of these fun events! We hope you enjoy the walk down memory lane.

The Bell

WHEATLEY HILLS GOLF CLUB   East Williston, N. Y.

Volume 3   FEBRUARY, 1962   No. 2

February 1962 issue

The club is blessed with some clever talent judging by the recent TV performances of **Sonny Mackney** and **Marilyn Frame**. A few weeks after Sonny exhibited skill on Make a Face show, Marilyn enjoyed a $4,800 windfall on Bill Cullen's The Price Is Right.

Ed Boyajian has had a distinguished career as a flier, having cut his flying teeth with the fabulous Charles Augustus Lindbergh.

October 1962 issue

John Adikes dropped a 3-wood for a deuce on the 17th while playing with **Henry Hallock, Joe Keller** and **Admiral F.D. Kirkland.**

Frank Caprise eagled on the 17th while **Lester Weidner, Sr., Joe Callahan** and **Al Munro** looked on; **Frank Caprise** eagled the ninth, when his 9-iron second shot located the cup while playing with **Bill Meyer** and **Mike Caprise. Andy Viola,** not to be outdone, eagled the 18th when his 2-iron second shot dropped as **Al Schrafel, Sr.** and two guests stood aghast.

OUR CHAMP AND CAST — Suzy Peters, displaying leg cast, was presented the championship trophy by Norah Heath following her fourth triumph in the title event. L. to r., are Helen Carroll, Helen Drucker, Norah, Suzy, Rita Guiney, runnerup and Sally Kollner.

Suzy Peters Captures Title; Rita Guiney 2nd

Suzy Peters, in spite of being handicapped by a cast on her right leg, captured the women's championship for the fourth time in the last five years — and the third in succession.

The 19-year-old Wells College student suffered a falling accident at her home. A fractured right leg failed to dampen her ardor when the time arrived for her to defend the crown she had won the season before.

Susy, cheerful and poised in spite of the heavy cast that at times caused her pain, posted a winning score of 260 for the 54-hole medal test. Rita Guiney, runnerup in 1964 when Frieda Meissner won the title, was again the bridesmaid with 285.

It was Suzy's second best winning score. Her 254 made in 1968 was her finest performance. She won in 1967 with 263 and, in dominating the event when she was 15 years of age in 1965, Suzy posted 274.

Helen Drucker won the crown in Class B with 309, with Helen Carroll second at 311. Sally Kollner came through with 353 to annex the Class C diadem, with Elme Valentine the runnerup with 356.

In Class A, Wyn Caprise was first day net winner with 71, with Nora Dowdell the second day leader with 75 and Selma Reese the third day victor with 76.

In Class B, the net winners were Norah Heath 77, Towney Miceli 77 and Dot Schaefer 73. In Class C, Fran Cornacchia 90, Alberta Evans 78 and Marge Loufek 84 were the daily winners.

Shirley Byczek was the putting prize winner with 94 strokes on the 54 greens.

The team of Helen Carroll, Helen Drucker, Ann Kelly and Alberta Evans finished first in the August 27 fourball. The combine of Gladys Parzini, Frieda Meissner, Nancy Evans and Kit Lanchantin was second.

Nora Dowdell won the August 6 competition, with Marianne Gardner and Elme Valentine the other prize winners. Marion Uhe led the August 20 tournament. Dot Schaefer and Sally Kollner also carried off prizes.

Gladys Parzini, Helen Harroll, Tess Smith and Edna O'Connell formed the winning fourball combine. Nancy De Matteis, Ethel Post, Marion Willard and Lil Miles finished second.

REPAIR MARKS ON GREEN

N. J., and Richard Olszewski, cousin of the groom, of Trenton, N. J.

SUSAN PETERS (CONNORS)

Susan Peters was the youngest club champion at a private club in Long Island. One year she won the woman's title with a cast on her leg.

WHEATLEY
WOMEN'S TOURNAMENT
EVENTS
1948

Wheatley Hills Golf Club
East Williston, L. I., N. Y.

ETIQUETTE

The pleasure of a majority of players is frequently destroyed by the unnecessary deliberation and slowness of a few. In recognition of that situation the following rules, regulations and definitions have been adopted and will be strictly enforced.

RULE I. A match which fails to keep its place on the course and loses one clear hole on the players in front **MUST** be passed. It is the duty of the players causing delay to promptly give notice to come through without waiting for a demand to be made.

RULE II. Players must assert their rights from those in front. A match which fails to assert its rights and keeps back another match must allow the latter to pass.

RULE III. Players looking for a lost ball must signal the players following to pass. Having given such signal they must stand aside and cease play until these players have passed and are out of range.

RULE IV. It is the duty of all players to replace divots.

RULE V. It is the duty of players to smooth over heel prints and club marks in traps; and to refrain from climbing the face of bunkers.

RULE VI. Players must not take caddies unless assigned by the Caddie Master, and shall not buy balls from caddies, or others on the course.

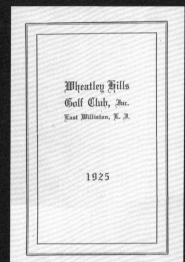

Wheatley Hills
Golf Club, Inc.
East Williston, L. I.

1925

Constitution.

Sec. 1. The name of the Club shall be the WHEATLEY HILLS GOLF CLUB, Inc. — **Article I.** Name

Sec. 1. The objects of the Club shall be the promotion and cultivation of social intercourse, the game of golf, and other athletic games and diversions among its members. — **Article II.** Object

Sec. 1. The membership of the Club shall consist of regular, associate, non-resident, life and honorary members. — **Article III.** Membership

Sec. 2. The regular members of the Club shall not exceed 250 in number and shall be limited to men of twenty-one years of age and upwards. The regular members shall be divided into two classes: Class A, to consist of all regular members who have subscribed for a membership certificate as provided in Article III, Section 3; Class B, to consist of all other regular members.

Sec. 3. The Club shall issue certificates of ownership in the real property of the Club hereafter acquired, to the regular members who shall subscribe therefor upon the payment of three hundred dollars ($300) to be made in such manner as the Board of Governors shall determine. The total number of certificates authorized and issued shall equal but shall not exceed the number of regular members, and any increase in such number

The reading of these two publications should bring a smile to your face.

Rules have always been an important part of club life and these writings are simply one example of the etiquette and expectations set forth for club membership.

The Bell

Wheatley Hills Golf Club - East Williston, N.Y.

Club News

We thought it might be fun to read some of the items that have been found in the pages of "THE BELL" over the years.

"Did You Know?" is an ongoing section of the publication. We have chosen a few fun facts for your reading enjoyment.

"Did You Know?"

On April 1, 1989, Walter F. Koetzle became the first member to span six decades of membership at Wheatley Hills Golf Club. Walter joined the club at age 30, in 1939. When he joined the club, the cost of his bond was $350.00.

In fiscal year 1964 between Nov. 1 and Oct. 31, members played 21,914 rounds of golf. By 1983, that number increased to 23,935 and today our count is still over 20,000 rounds for the 2012 season.

Caddie rates in 1969 were stated as: A single caddie for 18 holes will be paid a minimum of $6.00 and a double caddie will be paid a minimum of $12.00.

Dr. Charles Robinson won the club title the first year he became a member in 1934. Through the years, Doc ruled the fairways, winning many titles. His total silver mugs count is eight.

In 2002, Monsignor Joe Parks and Attorney Jack Barry were playing together as a twosome, which they had done every Wednesday for years. On the eighth hole, after the first shot Monsignor couldn't find his ball. When Jack putts out, he finds Monsignor's ball. You guessed it! A hole-in-one for Monsignor. There must be an angel living on the course because it was not his first.

Joseph Cornacchia, a longtime active member who has served on the Board, as well as on several committees, was the owner of two Kentucky Derby winners (Strike the Gold and Go for Gin) and was the printer of the mind-boggling "Trivial Pursuit" game.

Vol. 20, No. 3 — WHEATLEY HILLS GOLF CLUB — East Williston, N. Y. — April 1979

November 1970 issue

Judge Al Oppido, named to the Supreme Court by Governor Rockefeller last May, was re-elected as he polled the highest number of votes of the six candidates.

Hope and Howard Treiber, Lois and Frank Faruolo, Irene and Sam Clayton enjoyed fall golf at Hilton Head Island.

Tony Nocito and Tony Napoli went to Rome to compete in the annual Italian Pro-Am, which was favored by superb weather.

At Old Westbury Golf & Country Club, **Gil McNally** teamed with **Art Hirshberg, Ed Bergman** and **Dr. Henry Cohen** to score 62 and carry off third-place prizes in the PGA Pro-Member.

An article in the Hempstead Sentinel in 1917 stated that "because of a long waiting list and a demand for admittance to the club, it was voted to raise the membership to 250 and at the same time, the initiation fee was raised from $50 to $100."

A 1917 article in the Brooklyn Eagle stated that "Wheatley Hills Golf Club was on a paying basis for the first time in its short history. Members held an enthusiastic and optimistic meeting at the Crescent Athletic Club. The treasurer's report showed that a profit of $2400 was had on the year, which leaves the club more than $10,000 on the right side of the ledger. This was too much money for most of the members present, so plans were made to spend that sum and a few dollars more on needed improvements. The House Committee submitted a proposition for additions to the clubhouse, which will greatly increase the present facilities, giving additional locker room and sleeping accommodations for those members caring to stay overnight. An expenditure, ratified, of $3000 will pay for these improvements."

The Motor Parkway can be seen behind the golfer in the middle to just above the golfer on the right. If you look closely, you can see the power lines in the background.

The **Bell**

Wheatley Hills Golf Club

NOVEMBER 2008   *Recognizing 95 Years of Golf Traditions*

Frank Osanitch (second from left) and Bill Wigginton receive the MGA/Metlife Net Team Championship trophy from Metlife's Bob Pizzute (far left) and Ray Larkin, chairman of the MetNet Committee. They played the tournament at the Hempstead Country Club in 1992.

Did you know that the record for "Holes-in-One" for a season is 15 in 1999?

The Babe Zaharias Cancer Charity has been the most consistent charity supported by Wheatley Hills. The ladies started donating in 1964. The men joined in 2003. Our overall contributions through 2012 have been over $117,000. Congratulations to our members on this great accomplishment.

In 1975, the ladies voted that all new members must have six lessons with the pro.

In 2005, **Ro Abruzzi, Sherry Morris, Marcia D'Angelo and Sara Lotruglio** take third place at Regional Babe Zaharias at Glen Head CC, firing a gross 76.

In 1985, **Ginger Corcoran** became the first lady member to break 90 in her first year of membership.

Playing Times for Ladies
1965: Sunday, before 10 a.m. and after 2 p.m.
1971: Wednesday, before 11 a.m. and after 2 p.m.
        Sunday, after 12:30 p.m.
1982: Saturday/Sunday, noon

Wheatley Hills Ladies Organization has been a member of Women's Metropolitan Golf Association since 1917.

Junior golf for the young girls and boys is an important part of Wheatley Hills. Today, classes are conducted during the summer months by our assistant professionals. Junior boys and girls are grouped by age and taught the fundamental skills of the game. In addition, they review the ethics and courtesies of golf. Many of today's members have advanced from these classes to become competitive golfers.

1966 photo of our junior golfers: You may recognize a name or two.

Left to right, front row: Mike Caprise, Jr., Kevin Tulley, Sam Clayton and Frank Mormando

Second row: John Carroll, Robert Schrafel, Jim Dowdell, Jr., Brian Devaney, Jim Needham, Jr. and Jim Conway

RAYMOND "BARNYARD" BERNARD 1924-2005

Barnyard was a beloved employee whose service spanned 52 years. He was one of those special people who left his mark and is a part of Wheatley Hills history.

Mal Galletta won the North & South Men's Amateur Championship in 1944, at age 32 and then went on to win the MGA Senior Championship in 1984, at the grand young age of 72. He passed away in 2007, at the age of 95, with most of his scores still less than his age.

Alfred J. Kienzle was the general manager of the Motor Parkway in the early 1920s and it is his signature on the Motor Parkway ticket shown in Chapter 2. By the 1930s he was a member of Wheatley Hills and a contractor. In 1934, he is listed in a local paper as V.P. of the D.S. Wilson Development Corp. The firm built cabins, mainly around Lake Ronkonkoma. Since he was a member, it is very possible he built the cabin, as a gift to the club, and so they named it "Kienzle Cabin," in his honor.

Another bit of trivia about Mr. Kienzle is that he had a hole-in-one on the eighth hole in 1939 and had a tournament named for him in the 1950s (the A.J. Kienzle Memorial Tournament).

In the quarter-finals of the junior championship at Wheatley Hills Golf Club, Frank Stone defeated Ted D'Lyra, 2 and 1; Clint Hammond eliminated S. J. Mackney, 3 and 1; M. J. Brady Jr. defeated A. E. Roeder, 2 and 1 and A. J. Schrafel Jr. won by the same margin over Walter Horne . . . In the qualifying round of the A. J. Kienzle Memorial, Mike Caprice and Fred Head tied at 67 net . . . Fred had a gross of 71.

This article appeared in the Hempstead Paper in 1952.

This cup is on display at the club.

Alfred J. Kienzle, on the left, standing in front of one of the Motor Parkway gatekeepers' cottages.

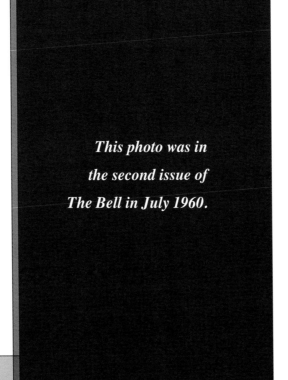

MEN'S / WOMEN'S Scorecard

Yards	Par	Hdcp	Hole	Art	Bill G-Schell	B Henning	T Petty	W-L-H-O	Yards	Par	Hdcp
342	4	12	1	5 5	5	9	10		322	4	12
366	4	9	2	4 6	6	6	6		366	4	10
215	3	14	3	4 6	5	5	4		215	4	16
546	5	2	4	5 7	8	6	6		500	5	2
501	5	6	5	6 7		7	7		455	5	6
187	3	15	6	5 4		4	5		142	3	18
505	5	4	7	7 7		6	6		450	5	4
167	3	17	8	4 4		4	3		167	3	14
380	4	8	9	5		5	7		380	4	8
3209	36	OUT		46		50	54		2997	37	OUT
181	3	16	10	5		5	5		181	3	15
435	4	5	11	5		8	5		400	5	5
524	5	3	12	5		8	11		479	5	3
320	4	13	13	4		6	5		320	4	11
159	3	18	14	4		6	5		159	3	17
595	5	1	15	7		8	8		555	5	1
340	4	11	16	4		5	5		340	4	7
401	4	7	17	4		5	5		360	4	9
368	4	10	18	5		5	5		268	4	13
3323	36	IN		43		50	54		3062	37	
6532	72	TOTAL		88		106	108		6059	74	
		HANDICAP									
		NET SCORE									

Local Rules

1. Foursomes and twosomes have equal rights, Saturdays, Sundays and Holidays. Matches in club competition have right of way.
2. Players shall not practice on any tee, fairway or green.
3. Starting at the tenth tee is permitted until 10 A. M. and between 12 and 2 P. M. Under no circumstances should a start be made at any other time.
4. The United States Golf Association and local rules govern play."
5. Ball striking wires overhanging ninth green may be replayed without penalty.
6. Out of bounds penalty is loss of distance only.
7. Out of bounds, stakes between 9th and 18th holes.
8. The faster match must pass the slower, no matter the number of players in the latter. This must be observed.

Please Replace Turf and Smooth Sand in Traps

Oct 22, 1952 —

BAD DAY

Wheatley Hills Golf Club

TOM PETTY
BOB HENNING — 18 HOLES
ME

4 HOLES — SCHFF
9 HOLES — BILL HANLEY

EAST WILLISTON, NEW YORK

Not what you would call a good day on the golf course for Mr. Scheff.

Perhaps it was best the group started out as a fivesome, since after the first four holes it was a foursome and after eight holes, Bill Hanley left the group and now it was only a threesome.

The "champion" of the day, October 22, 1952, was Howard Treiber, with an 88. It would appear Bob Henning and Tom Petty were winners too, just for finishing the round.

This photo was in the second issue of The Bell in July 1960.

LESTER HAS GOOD REASON FOR SMILING

Tournament chief Ted Peters, former president Pete McDermott and club treasurer John J. Sandhaas pose for our photographer with smiling Lester Weidner, who not only made his third ace with the ball he's holding, but came within inches of another on the 10th, a few days after taming the 185-yard 14th. Good work, Lester.

THE FIRE

Fire alarms went off in the local volunteer firehouses in the early morning hours of February 6, 1976. Within a very few minutes, the departments that responded knew they had a major fire on their hands.

The dedication and expertise of these highly trained volunteers is the reason Wheatley Hills clubhouse is still standing today. We will always be grateful for their untiring efforts that cold winter night.

The following narrative is taken from a letter to Wheatley Hills Golf Club members in 1976. Francis X. Sperl, then club president, wrote it.

WHEATLEY·HILLS·GOLF·CLUB
EAST WILLISTON
LONG ISLAND

Early in the morning of February 6, 1976 disaster struck Wheatley Hills Golf Club by way of fire.

Within a short time the Men's Locker Room and the Card Room were razed, the Bar and Grill Rooms destroyed, and extensive damage caused to the Kitchen and Dining Rooms. Except for the quick response of the neighboring fire departments and the professionalism with which they contained the damage, the fire threatened to level the entire Clubhouse.

Quickly the Board of Governors met to assess the damage and to arrange for repairs and refurnishing. The Board's prime consideration was with maintaining the character of the building in the rehabilitation and with keeping inconvenience to members at a minimum during the process. Fortunately we were able to secure the services of a professional consultant, familiar with our Clubhouse, who had authorative background in institutional modernization. Structural adjustments and decor were planned so as to maintain the Club's distinction and appeal to members.

From that day to the present the world of contractors, architects, suppliers and public adjusters became a part of the everyday life at Wheatley Hills Golf Club. All these people, plus the members of the staff and the Board of Governors, contributed substantially to the progressive refurbishing of the Club as depicted in the photographs which go to make up this brochure.

It is felt that you, the members, would appreciate receiving a pictorial report of what was certainly one of the most eventful years in the history of Wheatley Hills Golf Club.

Very truly yours,

Francis X. Sperl
President.

In the early morning hours of February 6, 1976 disaster struck Wheatley Hills Golf Club by way of fire.

Within a short time, the men's locker room and the card room were razed, the bar and grill rooms destroyed and extensive damage was caused to the kitchen and dining rooms. Except for the quick response of the neighboring fire departments and the professionalism with which they contained the damage, the fire threatened to level the entire clubhouse.

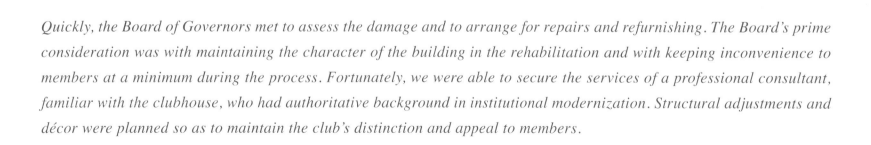

Quickly, the Board of Governors met to assess the damage and to arrange for repairs and refurnishing. The Board's prime consideration was with maintaining the character of the building in the rehabilitation and with keeping inconvenience to members at a minimum during the process. Fortunately, we were able to secure the services of a professional consultant, familiar with the clubhouse, who had authoritative background in institutional modernization. Structural adjustments and décor were planned so as to maintain the club's distinction and appeal to members.

From that day to the present the world of contractors, architects, suppliers and public adjusters became a part of the everyday life at Wheatley Hills Golf Club. All these people, plus the members of the staff and the Board of Governors, contributed substantially to the progressive refurbishing of the club as depicted in these photographs.

We are grateful for the tireless efforts of Vincent M. Massina, whose company rebuilt the clubhouse and had us open for the bicentennial celebration that summer.

Activities and Traditions

Many a good time has been experienced by the Wheatley Hills' members and their families over the past 100 years.

Dull moments are hard to find once you step inside the club. There is always something going on. It may be a group playing cards or watching a not-to-be-missed sports event. It could be enjoying a sumptuous lunch or dinner and of course, getting ready for the next round of golf.

The staff and management make sure that boring is not in their vocabulary and are always looking for new ways to entice you to visit the club and have a good time.

Over the last 100 years, there has been such a variety of activities it is impossible to cover them all, but the following pages highlight some great memories and lots of smiles and laughter.

Whether it was Hawaiian night, the Beatles, Christmas parties, amateur night, Halloween, fashion shows, card tournaments or the Fourth of July party, the club has centered around it all.

Hopefully, you will find a memory or two in these pages that resonate with you and your family.

Vol. II, No. 11   WHEATLEY HILLS GOLF CLUB — East Williston, N. Y.   November, 1970

Nick Mormando Wins Gin Rummy Title

By George Driscoll
Gin Rummy Chairman

Nick Mormando won the Gin Rummy Classic, defeating Bill Peters in the final. Nick, feeling all of "his Power", planned an early knockout and won it in the fourth round. Peters, badly staggered, failed to come out for the bell.

Al Schaeffner Wins Gin Rummy Classic

There was no generation gap in the annual Gin Rummy Classic. Al Schaeffner, who served as club president 26 years ago, 11 years after joining Wheatley Hills, emerged as the winner of the competition staged March 3 at the clubhouse.

The oldest contestant in the tournament, Al knocked out another erstwhile prexy, Bill Meyer, in the final. In the semis, Al stopped Tom Appel and Bill Neuman was eliminated by Meyer.

LEY HILLS GOLF CLUB — East Williston, N. Y.   March, 1973

60 Gin Buffs Compete In Spring Team Event

The annual Spring Gin Tournament, staged March 9, attracted 60 members. Three flights were staged, with no distinction being made.

In the first flight action, Jack Barry and Frank Baerenklau were the winners. Ted Peters and Al Schaeffner dominated the second flight and Fred Hill and Clarence Fuss took the third flight honors.

Dan Devaney Captures Spring Gin Rummy

Dan Devaney, who next year celebrates his silver anniversary as a club member, dominated the annual Spring Golden Crown Gin Rummy Championship on March 26.

In the final-round match, Dan repulsed the bid of Frank X. Sessa, chairman of the green committee. In their semifinal tests, Dan stopped Clarence Fuss and Sessa defeated Bob Hooper, golf chairman.

LEY HILLS GOLF CLUB — East Williston, N. Y.   April 1979

McElwain & Trabucchi Win Gin Rummy Final

Bill McElwain teamed with Aldo Trabucchi and captured top honors in the annual Spring Gin Rummy event held at the club last month. In the final round encounter, Frank Bush and Armin Kikel lost to the McElwain team.

"It was the tenacity of Trabucchi, plus the steady playing of McElwain that enabled the team to triumph," said Kikel.

Weiss and Schrafel Jr. Win Gin Rummy Classic

Frank Weiss and Al Schrafel Jr. stalked through a formidable field of opponents on February 7 to capture the top laurels in the annual Winter Gin Rummy Classic at the clubhouse.

Frank and Al, in the final round match, defeated Tony Kearshes and Bob Spinner. In the final of the Beaten Eight, Clarence Fuss and Fred De-Matteis turned back Bill Neuman and Raymond Backel.

Gin Rummy – A Staple at the Club

Gin rummy has been an activity that is enthusiastically pursued by a number of our members.

It provides an opportunity to test one's skill in the card room after 18 holes of golf or when Mother Nature is not cooperating.

We joke that players, when observing the play of their partners, can provide "expert" commentary after the hand has been played. It adds to the excitement.

Over the years, "Gin Rummy Classics" have been played to determine the "best" player or partners.

Mary Ann Tauhert Hits Series of 607

Mary Ann Tauhert, whose series of 542 leads the distaffers in the Wheatley Hills Golf Club Mixed Bowling League, rolled an amazing 607 to win a trophy in the Garden City Bowl League Championship.

June, 1964

BOWLING WINNER

Wynn Caprise proved the star of the Mixed League at Sheridan Academy, being high average for the distaffers with 137 and high game with 480. Viv Kramer won high game honors with 220. Among the men, President Mike Caprise was high average with 257, Jack Kollner high game with 165 and Cal Rafuse high series with 587. Jack Mallon's team of Viv Kramer, George Kramer and Barbara Leus won the honors with 107 wins and 58 losses. Ted Peters' team was second, Lou Schreoder's third, Mike Caprise's fourth, Jack Kollner's fifth and Cal Rafuse's sixth.

November, 1962

Lillian Frame Hits 194 In Bowling Opener

Bowling champ Lillian Frame showed the way to the Wheatley Hills Women's League in the opening matches held at Sheridan Lanes, Mineola.

After starting with a 164, Lillian rolled the high for the young season, a 194. Nancy De Matteis, who got off a fine 161 in the opening game, hit 182 in the second session to post the second high.

May, 1964

Treiber Agency Wins Bowling Title

The John Treiber Agency carried off the title in the Wheatley Hills Women's Bowling League at Sheridan with a ledger of 87½ wins and 42½ setbacks. Cornwall and Stevens took second with 75-55, with American Improved Products third with 68-62 and Schrafel Paper fourth with 65-65.

January, 1975

Gabe Cicerani Hits 605 for High Series in Mixed Bowling League

Gabe Cicerani is leading the Wheatley Hills Mixed Bowling League at Garden City Bowl with a series of 606. Vincent Massina is trailing with 572. Nora Dowdell is high gal with 541, with Towney Miceli second with 514.

Massina is high game with 234, with Ray Mrozack next at 222. Helen Louros is high with 205, with Viv Conte second with 201.

John Louros is high average with 173, with his wife, Helen, the top distaffer, with 153.

The Divots — Barbara Schrafel, Flo Howley, Pete Miceli, Bill Breen and John Louros — are leading with 101-51, with the Drivers — Nora Dowdell, Mary Knipfing, Alberta Evans, Dan Edlind and Les Howley — next at 88-66.

Lillian Frame, Jim Dowdell Lead in Bowling League

Lillian Frame and Jim Dowdell dominate the Wheatley Hills Golf Club Mixed Bowling League. Lillian, in fact, is not only tops in the distaff

January, 1975

Marie Mormando Hits 540 in Women's Bowling League

Marie Mormando, whose uncle Joe Falcaro, used to be world's bowling champion, is dominating the action in Wheatley Hills GC Women's League at Sheridan Academy. She took the lead in the race for series honors with 540, displacing Marilyn Frame, who had 533. Nora Dowdell had 525.

Marie also is high average with 159, one more than Nora and Josie Dihlmann. Marie Buckley fired a 206 to take the lead in the high game

category. Gilda Ireland, who in one series had 203 and 201 is tied for second at 203 with Mary Courtney.

The Faultless team of Caroline Oregelfinger, Rosalie Vigliorola, Flo Howley and Marie Mormando is in front of the standings with 102½-51½. The Achusnets — Mary Knipfing, Billie Price, Dee Conway and Nancy De Matteis trailed by eight points when this issue went to press.

Frame Chevvy Leads Ladies' League

The Frame Chevvy team of Edith de sa Rocha, Dot Schraefer, Alberta Evans and Lillian Frame hold the lead in the Wheatley Hills Golf Club Ladies' Bowling League at Sheridan Academy with 77 wins and 55 losses. Peter P. McDermott—Mary June Lahey, Carmella Foran, Matilda Stanford and Gladys Parzini—are second with 75½-56½, with Childs-Kramer next at 74½-57½. Rolling for Childs-Kramer are Betty Ryan, Ruth Paulsen, Ellie Hooper and Viv Kramer.

Sheridan Academy—Pat Haun, Jo Tully, Norah Heath and Wynn Caprise—ranks fourth with 73½-58½. Next in order are Meyer Chevvy, AIP, Schrafel Paper, Treiber Agency, Kollner Liquors and Cornwall & Stevens.

(Continued on Page Four)

Nick Mormando Inducted Into the International Bowling Museum and Hall of Fame.

Mormando's more than 50 years of dedication to the sport began when he borrowed $10,000 from his parents to purchase his first bowling center in 1948. Mormando earned election to the ABC Hall of Fame for his more than 20 years of service to the International Bowling Museum and Hall of Fame. Mormando was a major player in landing financial support from the bowling's commercial interests into the construction of the IBM/HF. During the formation stages of the St. Louis-based Museum and Hall of Fame, served on the site-selection, design and construction committees. He later served as IBM/HF President and Trustee, and he was instrumental in creating the Hall of Fames most important annual fundraising event, the Salute to Champions. The IBM/HF expressed its gratitude to Mormando by selecting him as its Salute to Champions honoree in 1994.

Bowling –
Winter Fun for Wheatley Hills Families

Whether it is single player or mixed league, Wheatley Hills-sponsored bowlers always have a fine showing. Good golfers must make good to great bowlers because our teams always are on the winning side of the ledger.

Wheatley Hills "On The Move"

WHEATLEY HILLS MEMBERS INVADE CARIBBEAN

Eighty-two members of the club are seen smiling for the photographer as they get ready to board the Eastern Air Lines jet on the recent Dorado Beach junket. Leo McGinity, Dr. John Stathis, Bill Condren and Jim Walsh won the Puerto Rico competition with a 62.

Dorado Fourball Paced By Mc Ginity's Team

Leo McGinity's combine of Dr. John Stathis, Bill Condren and former club president Jim Walsh won the Dorado Beach fourball during the recent golfing holiday enjoyed by 82 members of the club.

Christmas Fund For Employees

The traditional Christmas Fund for our loyal employees is now taking shape. Contributions to the fund from members wishing to reward the employees who have served them so well during the year may be delivered or mailed to the manager. Don't, please, overlook this matter. Get your check in early. Thanks.

REPAIR MARKS ON GREEN

Leo's team posted a 62, two strokes better than two other quartets. Walter Koetzle, George Kramer, Lou Wetzel and Al Schaeffner deadlocked at 64 for second with the combine of Ed Simpson, Bob Miller, Ted Rubsamen and Al Oppido.

Next, at 65, was the team of Lester Weidner, Sr., Stewart Warner, Gene Ciri, a guest of Stan Byczek's from Brookville and Frank Carberry. Bill Meyer, Bob Peterson, Vincent Massina and Tony Marra tied at 66 with Nick Ryan, Jerry Andrasick, Mike Grella and Jim Murphy. Bob Lahey, Bill Byrnes, George Beatty and L. Duemler checked in at 68.

In the better-ball competition, Ed Simpson and Stewart Warner won with 67, with Bill Grote and Ted Rubsamen second with 68. Jerry Andrasick and Gene Ciri tied for third at 71 w i t h George Sheehan and George Kramer.

Helen Franz led the distaffers with a net 73, with Vic Kramer second at 81 and Shirley Byczek third with 85.

In the men's individual event, Bill Grote won with 72, with Gene Ciri next at 73 and Ed Simpson tied at 74 with Stewart Warner.

In another fourball Stan Byczek, Bob Lahey, B i l l Condren and J. Lynch triumphed with 63. Next, at 65, was the team of Lester Weidner, George Kramer, L. Duemler and Al Schaeffner with 65.

Perfect flying weather made the jet trip via Eastern most delightful both ways. The Weather Man, too, was most cooperative during the stay

(Continued on Page Four)

The Dorado Beach Trip

In November 1964, Leo McGinity's team of Dr. John Stathis, Bill Condren and Jim Walsh won the Dorado Beach Four Ball during a golf holiday enjoyed by 82 members of Wheatley Hills.

The winning score was net 62 that topped all other competitors.

Never a group to sit still for very long, whether the trip be short (Manhattan Island), or long (Dorado Beach), the members find a way to share good times and make lasting friendships.

Dinner Dances

Party, Party, Party!

Masquerade Party 1936

Birthday Party circa 1940

Awards Dinner in the 1950s

Hawaiian Song

Amateur Night Stars

Fashions at Lunch 1996

Kids Just Want to Have Fun...

and they sure do at Wheatley Hills!

Traditions at Wheatley Hills

Jamie Kilmer, club pro;
Matt Dobyns; Charlie Bolling;
and Ben Orlowski, club
superintendent; savor the
winning moments after
Matt places first and
Charlie places second in the
Treiber Memorial in 2012.

THE TREIBER MEMORIAL

In 1981 Howard Treiber approached the Metropolitan PGA with a concept for a year end event. Mr. Treiber was a past president of Wheatley Hills Golf Club and a member of the local golf association boards who enjoyed a long running love affair with golf and especially the local professionals. His goal was to create a match play event that would be a culmination to the season, bringing professionals together in both a competitive and fraternal atmosphere that promoted the very best values of the game.

But, Howard Treiber's motives were not just rooted in a desire to create a new championship. He also enjoyed a very special feeling about Wheatley Hills Golf Club. He believed that Wheatley Hills embodied what a golf club was all about — a shot maker's delight of a unique course blending great par 3's with a variety of par 5's and 4's along with a membership and staff that loved the game and pride fully opened their doors to see golf at its finest. Wheatley Hills was also special in that the language of golf was spoken as fervently at the bar, in the cabin or around the lunch table as it was on the course itself Howard Treiber loved Wheatley Hills and felt it was a perfect setting to showcase the club, the golf course and the local professionals. It was always a welcoming site to approach the 18th green where past presidents and current members of the club, key staff, fellow professionals, friends and caddies would all gather along with the entire Treiber family to watch a match to its conclusion. Win or lose it was a time when Howard Treiber enjoyed seeing old golf buddies, making new friends and sharing his passion for golf with players and spectators alike.

In memory of his late brother Russell, Howard coined the event The Treiber Memorial. From its earliest days the championship created its own wonderful history. Three of the very first champions, Jim Albus, Larry Laoretti and Mike Joyce went on to amazing success on the Champions Tour with all three winning on the over 50 circuit and Albus and Laoretti each winning majors — The Senior Players Championship and the US Senior Open. All the top players would compete, loving the atmosphere and enjoying the format that minimized the disruption to Wheatley Hills' normal routines. Two former Wheatley Hills' pros have been successful in the event. Mike Gilmore, former head Pro, won in 1997 and Jon Kudysch, an Assistant Pro, won in 1986.

Ultimately, the Treiber Memorial took on an even more significant role in the Met PGA's schedule. In 1994, the event became the Treiber Memorial Tournament of Champions. Eligible winners of each of the area's major local championships were exempted into the field and ultimately, over a decade later, the format shifted from match play to the only stableford competition in the area. The change in format provided a more fitting conclusion to the Met PGA's Player of the Year point race as individual scores replaced the random nature of head to head matches. A Senior Division was added as the event chose to also recognize the contributions and playing skills of those who enjoyed serving the area and golf for years, just as the Treiber family has served the community for so long.

In our day to day world it is easy to lose sight of what makes golf so special. Wheatley Hills and The Treiber Memorial are an annual reminder of the people and venue that have created this wonderful legacy.

The Treiber Memorial Past Champions

2012 Matt Dobyns	2001 Bob Bigonette	1990 Darrell Kestner
2011 Carl Alexander	2000 Tim Shifflett	1989 Bruce Zabriski
2010 Charlie Meola	1999 Paul Glut	1988 Tom Gleeton
2009 Greg Bisconti	1998 Ralph Garofano	1987 Jack McGown
2008 Frank Bensel	1997 Mike Gilmore	1986 Jon Kudysch
2007 Mark Brown	1996 John DeForest	1985 Craig Watson
2006 Jim Wahl	1995 Darrell Kestner	1984 Jim Albus
2005 Charlie Bolling	1994 Darrell Kestner	1983 Larry Laoretti
2004 Colin Amaral	1993 Austin Straub	1982 Jim Albus
2003 Jim Thompson	1992 Darrell Kestner	1981 Mike Joyce
2002 Robert Deruntz	1991 Ed Burke	

Fourth of July Annual Picnic and Fireworks

On the Fourth of July we celebrate not only our independence, as a nation, but the foundation of the family.

The July Fourth party is about our families and especially the kids, young and old.

Grilling, music, fireworks and games are the rule of the day.

The Needham family, longtime members, line up the grandchildren for their annual Fourth of July picnic photo.

CHARITIES - A WHEATLEY TRAIT

Wheatley Hills has a long history of supporting local and other charities.

Long Island Caddie Scholarship Fund

The Long Island Caddie Scholarship Fund, established in 1962 by George Sands, provides need-based financial assistance to deserving young men and women who have worked as caddies or in other jobs in service to golf, assisting in the pursuit of a higher education.

In the 50-year history of the fund, over 800 college scholarships have been awarded, representing a financial commitment of over $3 million. In the most recent fiscal year, ended October 31, 2011, 22 scholarships were awarded, for a financial commitment of $176,000.

The Long Island Caddie Scholarship Fund is supported by donations from member clubs of the Long Island Golf Association, allied associations, corporations, foundations and individuals.

For many years, Frank Faruolo, Wheatley Hills member and past president (1974), was an active supporter and served as secretary to the group.

In the past 20 years, our club has donated upward of $150,000. In that time, 40 Wheatley caddies have been selected to receive awards. It has been established that we are one of the most generous clubs on Long Island in support of this charity. We have included four of our winners here.

Long Island Caddie Scholarship Fund Winners

John Flynn

James D. Reidy, III

John Paul Igoe

Greg Brescia

The club has always embraced organizations and causes that work to support those in need.

Some of those we have supported:

§ Coma Recovery   §   The Seeing Eye Dog Foundation   §   The Maurer Foundation 1998
§ Make-A-Wish Foundation 1999   §   American Red Cross   §   Corpus Christi Church
§ St. Aidan's Church

LEAD THE WAY

Lead the Way Fund, Inc. was
established in 2007 to support
disabled U.S. Army Rangers
and their families. Wheatley Hills has been involved since 2011
and to date we have contributed over $23,000 to the group to help
ease the financial burdens of these families.

ADOPT A PLATOON

It is dedicated to serving deployed U.S. service men
and women, ensuring they are not forgotten. Wheatley Hills has contributed $10,000 to them in 2011.

FOLDS OF HONOR

The Annual Patriot Golf Day held over Labor Day weekend is another charity
strongly supported by Wheatley Hills. In 2012, $4000 alone was contributed, and
in the previous six years, over $12,000 found its way in the support of our military.

BABE "Z"

Since 1964, thousands of dollars have been given in support of this cancer charity toward finding a
cure and helping survivors. Over the years, we have contributed over $117,000 to the organization.

The generosity of our members is well documented in their support of those in need.

Annual Long Island Golf Association Dinner

This photo is from the 1930 dinner at the Hotel New Yorker.

ANNUAL DINNER OF LONG ISLAND GOLF ASS'N
HOTEL NEW YORKER - DEC. 4, 1930

EMPIRE
PHOTOGRAPHERS
N.Y.

Father's Day Tournament

The annual Father's Day Tournament is another Wheatley Hills tradition that encourages family fun and happy memories. It is a grand day when dads get to share time and stories with their offspring.

Twilight Golf

Twilight golf is more of a social happening than a competition. Husbands and wives and boyfriends and girlfriends form teams to play in a nine-hole tournament using the alternate shot format. A lot of unhappy wives or girlfriends are not pleased when their partner's shot goes astray. This often leads to accusations, but more importantly an evening of laughter. All is forgiven when they sit down to dinner with their fellow competitors and reminisce about the fun they just had.

The Wheatley Hills Golf Club has made it a tradition to volunteer
for the USGA Championships when played in the area.

This was evident in 2002 and in 2009 when the volunteers served
with distinction as marshals during the tournaments.

At both events, the crew was placed in charge of the 10th Hole — 508 Yard Par 4.

Our U.S. Open Marshals and Hospitality Committee 2009 Team included

Park Adikes, Patricia Adikes-Hill, Leo Albano, Toni Albano, Joseph Amato, James Anziano, Joe Araneo, Jeff Arends, David Bahr, Anita Bjork, John Cahalane, Gerald Calder, Craig Campbell, Robert Carswell, Chris Caruso, Frank Cashin, Kevin Cashin, Doug Christ, Robert Codignotto, William Coles, John Colleary, James Corda, John Costello, Frederick Courtney, Jr., Peter Courtney, Frank Danisi, Ken Dean, Martin Delaney, John Donohue, Nick Donohue, Jesse Dowdell, Carl Eckhoff, Brian Fendt, James Fendt, John Fitzgerald, Anthony Gallagher, Peter Ganley, Louis Garcia, Michael Hagony, Carl Hanson, Patrick Hayes, Christopher Hilton, Kristina Hilton, Ted Hutchison, Vincent Infantino, Thomas Jacoberger, Edmund Jules, Sandy Kambourian, Bernard Kennedy, Lisa Kennedy, George Krug, Chrissy Lavelle, Michael Lavelle, Matt Lavelle, Tony Lotruglio, Sara Lotruglio, Maria Lynn, Robert Lynn, Steve Marman, Vincent Massina, James Mayo, Charles McGorty, Kevin McMorrow, Joyce Merzbacher, Mark Merzbacher, Richard Merzbacher, Richard Meyer, Thomas Mojo, Sherry Morris, Jeffrey Mullhall, Gail Mulligan, Kacee Mulligan, Kevin Mulligan, James Myers, Michael Nikolai, Diane O'Donnell, Philip O'Donnell, John Pascale, Louis Quaglia, John Quigg, Rosemarie Quigg, Norma Roberto, Robert Roberto, Arthur Rommel, Samuel Rozzi, Rose Marie Santilli, Charles Schmitt, Jane Schrafel, Thomas Schrafel, Michael Shelley, Robert Schields, Matthew Smith, Samantha Smith, Richard Taylor, Denise Vascellaro, Perry Vascellaro, Francis Vecchione, Bob Vissichelli, Robert Wellner, Maureen Wellner, Joe Wengler

U.S. Open 2002 Volunteers included many of the people above and the following:

David Bonagura, Daniel Carbone, Archie Cheng, Kenneth Coyle, Neil Connors, Joe Dolazel, Scott Heaney, Robert Lynn, Maria Lynn, Dr. Arthur Marchiano, Paul May, Joseph Mazza, Robert McBride, Chris McTiernan, William Meunier, John Murro, James Paterson, Jeanne Ricigliano, Richard Spinelli

BOARD OF GOVERNORS

T he Board of Governors has been the governing body of the club since its first official act of leasing some farmland to build the course they envisioned.

Every time a decision was needed, the Board was there to act. Whether it was the hiring of Devereaux Emmet to design the golf course or dealing with the powerful master builder, Robert Moses, the men who formed the Board always placed the best interests of the club first and worked tirelessly to implement the best result for the majority of the membership.

They were tough. When the budget was tight they were frugal, when the money was available they spent it wisely.

When the club experienced its greatest tragedy, the 1976 fire, the rebuilding and refurbishing effort led by the Board was exceptional. Many believed we would not have a clubhouse for the 1976 season, but we were open for the annual Fourth of July celebration.

Through a collaborative committee structure, the Board of Governors has followed a tradition of delivering a great golfing experience for members, while consistently exercising sound financial discipline. We are well positioned for the next 100 years thanks to the dedicated group of members who have served on the Board of Governors and its committees.

2013 BOARD OF GOVERNORS

Standing left to right: **John Horan, Michael Belcher, Bob Palmieri, Robert Domini, Chris Sauvigne, Dr. Glenn Muraca, Patrick Hayes, Leo Albano**

Seated left to right: **Kevin McAndrew, Frank Caliendo, Anthony Carillo, President Bill Poisson, C.V. McGinity, Frank D'Ambra, Richard Kearns**

CLUB PRESIDENTS

1914-1918	RICHARD TURNER	1947-1948	FRANKLIN E. DEVLIN
1919-1920	E.B. DAMS	1949-1951	JOHN J. SCHLEIF
1921-1922	FRANK TOMLIN	1952-1954	WILLIAM T. SLADER
1923-1924	ARTHUR P. LEE	1955-1958	WILLIAM J. WALTERS
1925-1927	WILLIAM J. ROONEY	1959-1960	JAMES W. WALSH
1928	CHARLES E. MEEK	1961-1962	ANDREW J. O'ROURKE
1929	CONRAD A. MANSON	1963	WILLIAM T. HAZELTON
1930-1932	DAVID WOOD	1964-1966	MICHAEL A. CAPRISE
1933-1934	JOSEPH S. MORGAN	1967-1969	HOWARD F. TREIBER
1935-1937	JOHN SHERMAN MEYERS	1970	WILLIAM P. MEYER
1938-1940	HERBERT HAPPERSBERG	1971	WALTER F. KOETZLE
1941-1942	CLINTON M. FINNEY	1972	ROBERT J. HOOPER
1943-1944	RUDULPH MATTIS	1973	FRANCIS X. SESSA
1945	PETER P. MCDERMOTT	1974	FRANK J. FARUOLO, JR.
1946	ALOYSIUS F. SCHAEFFNER	1975	ANTHONY NOCITO

CLUB PRESIDENTS

1976	FRANCIS X. SPERL	1993	ARTHUR DOHM
1977	VINCENT M. MASSINA	1994	JOHN A. NEEDHAM
1978	ALFRED SCHRAFEL, JR.	1995	THOMAS CHRISTMAN
1979	WILLIAM NOLAN	1996	DR. ARTHUR MARCIANO
1980	RICHARD D. FRAME	1997	LEO ALBANO
1981	JOHN A. NEEDHAM	1998	JAMES ANZIANO
1982	JOHN E. WILSON	1999-2000	VINCENT C. MASSINA
1983-1984	JACK WRIGHT	2001-2003	FRED J. CARILLO
1985	WILLIAM TYREE	2004-2005	MATTHEW L. SMITH
1986	PATRICK PURCELL	2006	CHRISTOPHER SAUVIGNE
1987	RONALD CROFTON	2007-2008	JAMES D'ADDARIO
1988-1989	ALDO TRABUCCI	2009	ARCHIE CHENG
1990	EDWARD MUNSON	2010-2011	C.V. MCGINITY
1991	ANDREW RAFUSE	2012-2013	WILLIAM POISSON
1992	JOHN TREIBER		

CURRENT MEMBERS
WHO HAVE SERVED ON THE BOARD OF GOVERNORS

Park T. Adikes 1975

Leo Albano 1993-1998, 2011-2013

James Anziano 1993-1998

Michael Belcher 2011-2013

Gerald Calder 2010-2012

Frank Caliendo 2012-2013

Daniel Caniano 2003-2008

Fred J. Carillo 1998-2003

Anthony Carillo 2010-2013

Archie Cheng 2004-2009

Thomas Christman 1991-1996

John Colleary 2005-2010

James D'Addario 1998-2004, 2006-2008

Gary DeRosa 2005-2010

Arthur Dohm, Sr., 1989-1994

Robert Domini 2009-2013

Paul Duffy 1999-2004

Dominick Foresto 1993-1996

Peter Ganley 2003-2008

Dr. Cono Grasso 1984-1989

Patrick Hayes 2009-2013

John Horan 2011-2013

Michael J. Joyce 1999-2004

Richard P. Kearns 1990-1996, 2013

Walter Kirby 2004-2009

Frank LaVacca 2001-2006

Jack Lynch 2007-2012

Robert P. Lynn, Jr. 1995-2000

Stanley Mackney 1976-1982

Leonard Marinello 1998-2004

Vincent M. Massina 1972-1977

Robert Massina 1994-1996

Vincent C. Massina 1995-2000, 2004-2006

William McDonald 2007-2009

William McElwain 1982

Leo McGinity 1989-1994

C.V. McGinity 2009-2013

Kevin McMorrow 2006-2011

Brandon Neligan 1989-1995

Richard Meyer 2006-2009

Thomas Mojo 1997-2002

Nicholas Mormando 1996-1998

Paul Morra 1991-1996

Raymond Mrozack 1986-1988

Glenn Muraca 2011-2013

John Murro 2004-2009

John Needham 1976-1980, 1993-1994

Dr. William Noble 1992-1997

W. Warren Nolan 1974-1979, 1987-1989

Robert Palmieri 2010-2013

William Poisson 2010-2013

Patrick Purcell 1982-1986

Andrew Rafuse 1986-1991, 2001-2003

Christopher Sauvigne 1997-2002, 2005-2007, 2009, 2011-2013

Alfred Schrafel, Jr. 1972-1978,1983-1985, 1993-1998

Robert Shields 1988-1991

Matthew Smith 1999-2005

Richard Taylor 2005-2010

James Totaro 1998-2003

John Treiber 1986-1992, 2008-2010

Dr. Joseph Troisi 1976-1981

Perry Vascellaro 1999-2005

The dedication of such members has made Wheatley Hills Golf Club.

WHEATLEY HILLS WOMEN'S GOLF ASSOCIATION
PAST CLUB CHAIRLADIES

Selma Reese 1965	Mary Knipfing 1979 - 1980	Sherry Morris 1997 - 1998
Lillian Frame 1966	Eileen Breen 1981 - 1982	Eileen Needham 1999 - 2000
Jane Carberry 1967	Carolyn Orgelfinder 1983	RoseMarie Santulli 2001 - 2002
Mary Sparrow 1968	Margaret Fiducia 1984 - 1985	Katie Zarghami 2003 - 2004
Nora Heath 1969 - 1970	Mary Ann Tauhert 1986 - 1987	Maureen Kearns 2005 - 2006
Dorothy Schafer 1971 - 1972	Josie Dihlmann 1988 - 1989	Lisa Kennedy 2007 - 2008
Marianne Gardner 1973 - 1974	Evy Munro 1990 - 1992	Ro Abbruzzi 2009 - 2010
Mary Stathis 1975 - 1976	Paula Christman 1993 - 1994	Christy Lavelle 2011 - 2012
Millicent Lohrand 1977 - 1978	Norma Roberto 1995 - 1996	Maria Lynn 2013

"We may be a small group, but we have a lot of spirit."

We apologize for not having a record of the names of the ladies who were chairladies before 1965.

Their dedication and energy to the club's success is no less honored than the names that appear above.

PETER P. MCDERMOTT | 1888-1965

A FORCE IN THE GOVERNANCE AT WHEATLEY HILLS

In every organization, there are people who are respected as natural leaders. Usually this person has a powerful personality and his influence is recognized by his associates.

Peter P. McDermott was such a person. Peter joined Wheatley in 1927 and passed away in 1965. He served as club president in 1945 and served on the Board of Governors from 1939 to 1953. During that time, he exerted strong influence within the club on governance and membership matters.

It was said that "Peter P." was Wheatley Hills in that era. A situation resulting in Peter P.'s disfavor could prevent a membership or terminate a membership. During his time at Wheatley Hills, his strength set the standard of behavior for the membership.

The story is told that each week when he dined, it was considered an "honor" to sit at HIS table, which faced the TV. Peter P. was a fan of the TV series "Bonanza." During the broadcast, no one dared to channel surf or change the channel for even a second. However, on occasion, an unsuspecting member would violate "the code" and the consequence was not pleasant.

He is remembered for his unwavering leadership during the very difficult war years and steering the club to success in the growth years that followed. To honor his memory and to recognize the esteem of his fellow members for his 38 years at Wheatley, the Senior Club Championship was named after "Peter P."

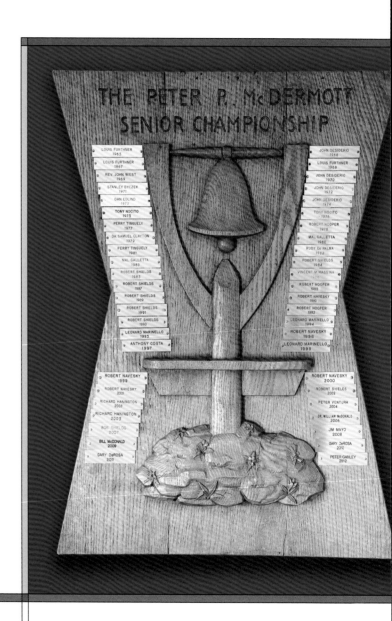

ROBERT J. HOOPER | 1928-2012

He was truly an extraordinary man. He was a friend and an inspiration to all who knew him, played golf with him or served with him on the many assignments he involved himself with at Wheatley Hills.

Completing a successful high school career as a golfer from Jamaica High School, Bob was offered the opportunity to join Wheatley Hills Golf Club. He was elected a junior associate member in 1948. He remained in that status until he turned 30 in 1958 and was approved as a regular member.

His competitive spirit came through in 1972 when he was playing in the prestigious Havemeyer Tournament. Down five holes with six holes to play, Bob executed several fine shots that turned the tide and gave him a 1-up victory on the 18th hole.

Bob was extremely active in the club and was on the Board of Governors and served for 13 years, in some capacity, between 1967 and 1990. His positions were the following:

1971 Board of Governors - Vice President | 1972 Board of Governors - President
Executive Committee - Chairman | House Committee - Chairman/Member
Entertainment Committee - Member | Membership Committee - Chairman/Member
Golf Committee - Chairman/Member | LIGA President - 1974-1975

As an individual or with a partner, Bob won a variety of tournaments, including three Senior Championships (1978, 1998, 1992) in the 60 years he was active at Wheatley.

Bob became a senior member in 2003, at age 75, but continued to play lots of great golf. During his senior years, he loved playing from the forward tees because, as he said, "I had a good chance of getting on the green in regulation."

His many friends at Wheatley will acknowledge how he lit up a room when he walked in. He was generous and he was friendly. In one 11-year stretch, he purchased 77 sets of irons, paying top dollar, and then gave them away or sold them for much less than what they cost him. Here is the real oddity: His decision to get rid of the new clubs was often made after only one round, part of a round or after a couple of swings. Once he lost interest in the clubs, it was sayonara.

Bob was at his best when he was the master of ceremonies at club events. Bob's needles were sharp, but never hurtful. His job was to make sure everyone had a good time.

Today, every one of his friends has a Bob story. However, one link in all his stories being told is that he made us feel happy in his presence. Bob passed away in 2012, but his stories and admiration still live on.

Anniversary Book Committee & Contributors

Park Adikes

*John J. Brennan

Anthony Carillo

Jay Carrieri

Gary DeRosa

Chris Hass

Jamie Kilmer

Sherry Morris

*Ted Peters

Matt Smith

Carol Taylor

John Treiber

Special Mention

James Anziano

Morton Bouchard

Katie Brophy

Nicole Ciaramella, USGA

James D'Addario

Ken Dean

James E. Dowdell, Jr.

Nancy Evans

Lynn Francis

Peter Ganley

Marilyn Gobel

Howard Kroplick

Sara Lotruglio

Stanley Mackney

Tom Mojo

Jeff Mulhall

Ben Orlowski

Dr. William Quirin

Steve Rabideau

Joseph Ryan

John Siebert

Steve Smith, LIGA

Lou Solferino

Rosemarie Torisi

William Wigginton

Nancy Zolezzi

Chairman

Perry C. Vascellaro

Co-Chairmen

Richard P. Kearns

John A. Needham

Staff

Jean Abate

Pat Bartlett

Ilene Madden

Patrice Flerx

Kathleen Grandon

Mary Jean Murphy

Editorial Assistant

Kerrie Stouges

Professional Photographers & Photo Credits

Art Ciccone - Golf Shots, Inc.

Pageant Photographers

Long Island Golf Association

Long Island Golf News

Long Island Motor Parkway Preservation Society

Geoffrey S. Cornish

Bob Valentine

Ronald E. Whitten

PGA TOUR

Metropolitan Golf Association

The Friends of Bobby Jones

The Babe Zaharias Foundation

Proclamation

Whereas; The East Williston Board of Trustees proudly join the Residents of the Incorporated Village of East Williston as they pay special tribute to the Members of The Wheatley Hills Golf Club, and

Whereas; The Wheatley Hills Golf Club was Incorporated on May 13, 1913 and was purchased from the A.H. Titus Farm Estate, and

Whereas, A building designed by J.H. Phillips was dedicated on November 18, 1926, suffered serious damage from a February 6, 1976 fire and was successfully restored to its current splendor, and

Whereas; The Historic Bell outside the clubhouse was used by several generations of the Titus Family to summon their farm hands for meals, and

Whereas; The Historic Vanderbilt Motor Parkway once divided the Golf Course into almost two equal parts

Now, Therefore; The Mayor and Board of Trustees do Hereby Proclaim that this 13th Day of May in the Year Two Thousand and Thirteen be Declared Wheatley Hills Golf Club Centennial Celebration Day in the Incorporated Village of East Williston.

_____
Mayor

A SNAPSHOT OF OUR HUMBLE BEGINNINGS

Emil A. Gunther,
Club Champion 1926

Below: As early as April 1916,
monthly bar sales exceeded food sales!

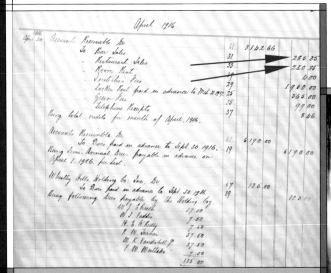

The current dining room (note high ceilings) was once the reading room

An early photo of the cabin

Frank Rand takes a swing in a 1929 tournament.

These photos have been preserved over the years and are on display at the club. Unfortunately, we are unable to identify all of the members or occasions.

Two Wheatley Hills icons, Jack Mallon and The Bell